Praise for *52 W...*
Your Smartphone Obsessed Kid

"If you're tired of being upstaged by a small rectangle made of glass and plastic, Jonathan McKee has the advice you need! Whether your pre-teen can't stop watching YouTube clips or Netflix or you're worried your older teen's most meaningful social interaction is with avatars on his phone or tablet, this book is a much-needed lifeline. Jonathan McKee also offers wise counsel for a variety of tough tech situations, and his suggestions are both innovative and completely doable."

—Shaunti Feldhahn, Social Researcher, National Speaker,
and Bestselling Author of *For Women Only*

"In a world where most parents feel frustrated by their kids' enslavement to social media and technology, Jonathan provides plenty of practical ideas to help parents create a climate of communication where kids actually put their phones down and engage in meaningful conversation."

—Doug Fields, Author of More than
50 Books Including *7 Ways to Be Her Hero*

"Jonathan McKee understands kids and this culture like few people I know. He is also passionate about helping parents find meaningful connection times with their kids. There are opportunities to engage, connect, and bond deeper on every page. The bonus questions at the end of every connection topic are easy to get parents and kids talking and sharing life. I highly recommend this book."

—Jim Burns, PhD
President, HomeWord
Author of *The Purity Code* and *Teaching Your Children Healthy Sexuality*

"Ya gotta love a guy who, speaking from a thoroughly researched standpoint plus personal experience teaching parenting workshops and herding teens (but heaven forbid, not simultaneously), understands the magical powers of cookie dough in drawing polar opposite fam members together in a kitchen and opening up conversation. There's nothing not to love about this book."

—Debora M. Coty, Humorist, Speaker, Award-Winning Author of
Numerous Inspirational Books Including *Too Blessed to be Stressed*

"*52 Ways to Connect with Your Smartphone Obsessed Kid* may have been written for parents, but it's a must-read for all of us. Thankfully, Jonathan McKee doesn't offer a hopeless message that all is lost unless we destroy our smartphones and turn our backs on technology. Instead, he gives us simple, memorable ways we can use our devices to strengthen our relationships instead of letting our tech toys run the family show. I'll be giving copies to my kids who are raising my grands in our wired-up world."

—Shellie Rushing Tomlinson, Author of *Heart Wide Open*

"If you're tired of seeing just the top of your kid's head bent over a smartphone, Jonathan McKee's new book, *52 Ways to Connect with Your Smartphone Obsessed Kid*, was written for you. . .and me. . .as he challenges parents (and grandparents) to examine the example we provide and encourages us we are not powerless to change the tide. . . . This book is one I'll buy for my adult children as well, as my grandsons are on the journey into a world very different than the one in which I raised my sons. Jonathan's book is long overdue."

—Deb DeArmond, Author of *Don't Go to Bed Angry. Stay Up and Fight!*

"Jonathan McKee has done it again! He's provided a timely tool for any parent looking to understand their children better in an increasingly technological age. Jonathan's candidness about his experiences with his own kids and the practical tips, questions, and research he's provided are bound to give any parent who reads this book the tools they have been looking for to connect with their kids on a deeper level. This book definitely has me thinking about how to create a climate of conversation with my own kids. So put down your smartphone and pick up this book!"

—Magdalene John, Co-Host, "100 Huntley Street"

"I regularly find that parents want help but don't know where to find the good stuff. So much parenting advice is fear-based and impractical. But Jonathan's gift to us is that he writes to parents from the intersection of hopeful parenting and practical ideas."

—Mark Oestreicher, Author of Many Books, Including *A Parent's Guide to Understanding Teenage Brains* and *Understanding Your Young Teen*

"Jonathan gives every parent a set of strategies to navigate the smartphone battlefield. *52 Ways to Connect with Your Smartphone Obsessed Kid* provides you with three wins: connect with your kids in the on-line world they know and love, steer your whole family away from damaging habits, and become an informed model of proper technology use."

—Hettie Brittz, Author of *(un)Natural Mom— Why You Are the Perfect Mom for Your Kids*

"Jonathan McKee has done it again! In *52 Ways to Connect with your Smartphone Obsessed Kid*, he has given parents a roadmap for relationship success with their kids. Jonathan shares important research on the overuse of screens and devices while combining his love of teens, respect for parents, and easy humor in each practical scenario offered to solve this universal challenge. A winning combination!"

—Carrie Abbott, President, The Legacy Institute, Radio Host, Speaker and Author

"As someone who speaks professionally to companies about managing distractions in a constantly connected workplace, I'm continuously asked for a resource from people on how to handle these issues with their kids. Jonathan's book is the resource I've been seeking for years. Not only will I recommend it, but I plan to adopt many of the strategies when I walk through the threshold of my home."

—Curt Steinhorst, National Speaker, President, Promentum Group

"Parents' concerns about their kids' screen use often lead to anxiety-based control through contracts, apps, and filters. The result is usually alienated kids who haven't learned self-control. Jonathan McKee will inspire and equip you with practical tools to build connection and influence with your kids, as you guide them toward true responsibility and wisdom with their cell phones and screens."

–Lynne Jackson, Co-Founder of Connected Families and Coauthor of *Discipline that Connects with Your Child's Heart*

How to Engage with Kids
Who Can't Seem to Pry Their
Eyes from Their Devices

52 Ways to Connect

with Your

Smartphone Obsessed Kid

JONATHAN MCKEE

SHILOH RUN  PRESS
An Imprint of Barbour Publishing, Inc.

Print ISBN 978-1-63409-707-9

eBook Editions:
Adobe Digital Edition (.epub) 978-1-63409-888-5
Kindle and MobiPocket Edition (.prc) 978-1-63409-889-2

The author is represented by, and this book is published in association with, the literary agency of WordServe Literary Group, Ltd., www.wordserveliterary.com.

Published by Shiloh Run Press, an imprint of Barbour Publishing, Inc., P.O. Box 719, Uhrichsville, Ohio 44683, www.shilohrunpress.com

Our mission is to publish and distribute inspirational products offering exceptional value and biblical encouragement to the masses.

 Member of the
Evangelical Christian
Publishers Association

Printed in the United States of America.

Acknowledgments

I wouldn't be writing this book if God hadn't opened the door for me to do so. It's only by His provision and grace that I am able to share any wisdom or experience. Anything good in this book is from Him, not me.

My wife, Lori, deserves so many thanks for this book. My kids grew up and headed off to school literally during the writing of this book. So any time pounding away at this project was time away from Lori during this new "empty nest" stage. Thanks for enduring through this process, Lori. You know you're my favorite!

Thanks to Kelly at Barbour Publishing, who spearheaded this book and is the one who really made it happen. Thanks for what you do, Kelly! I love working with you and look forward to our future projects.

Thanks to Greg Johnson, my agent and friend. You rock! I wouldn't even have this opportunity with Barbour had you not introduced us.

Thanks to Colleen Johnson, Phillip Ball, Michelle, Layton Dutton, and many of my other blog readers for helping me brainstorm about many of these ideas. It's such a help to hear from parents and youth workers who are on the front lines daily, navigating real life with teenagers. Thanks also to the countless readers who screened this book for me in its early stages. Your feedback was priceless.

And no thanks to you, Pip, my dog, for incessantly getting up from your spot, making noise, constantly disobeying, and driving me nuts as I tried to write this book. Yet you watched over Lori when I traveled, so *you totally redeemed yourself*!

Contents

Being Smarter
Than the Smartphone

"I can't get my daughter to look up from her phone and actually talk with me."

I hear this almost every weekend as I finish teaching one of my parent workshops. Moms and dads approach me and ask me how to connect with their tech-obsessed kids. Not so coincidentally, I'm experiencing the same struggle with my own kids. The smartphone is becoming a growing source of frustration, vying for everyone's attention.

Two hours later, I'll speak to a room full of teenagers. As I hang out with them afterward, inevitably I'll hear, "My mom and dad don't understand. All they do is nag me all the time. It's not like I'm out dealing drugs or driving drunk!"

It's interesting being in the unique position of hearing regularly from parents *and* from teens. Week after week, I hear the same thing. Parents regularly complain, "My kids spend too much time staring at their stupid phones!" And teenagers always protest, "My mom and dad won't let up about my phone!"

So who is right?

Last month my youngest daughter asked me honestly, "Dad, you don't think I spend too much time on my phone, do you?"

She had heard all the hype about "too much time on screens." You probably have too:

- *Today's thirteen- to eighteen-year-olds spend about nine hours (eight hours, fifty-six minutes) on entertainment media per day, excluding time spent at school or doing homework.* Common Sense Media did the extensive research in 2015. When you add up the time today's teens devote to TV, music, social media, video games, and all the personal time on their mobile devices, the numbers add up to more than a full-time job. And guess which device they're clocking the most hours on?

- *Screens hinder sleep.* In a recent study by the National Sleep Foundation, more than half of parents said their fifteen- to seventeen-year-olds routinely get only seven hours of sleep, or less, though the recommended amount for teens is eight and a half to ten hours. Why? Sixty-eight percent of these teens keep an electronic device on all night.

- *Screens can make your grades drop.* A brand-new study by Michigan State University followed five hundred MSU students, monitoring their academic performance as professors competed with smartphones, laptops, and other devices to get participants to engage. "The more they relied upon their gadgets as a distraction—even if it was to undertake quasi-relevant activities such as reading the news—the further their grades fell," the study states.

- *Screens are a new playground for bullying.* Gossip has just been given a turbo boost. Roughly 43 percent of teens have been harassed online (with about 25 percent of them claiming to have suffered more than one instance of it). Girls are twice as likely to be victims of cyberbullying, compared to boys, and, sadly, they are twice as likely to commit it, as well. Not surprisingly, kids who've endured cyberbullying are much more likely to attempt suicide than those who haven't. And parents are overwhelmingly unaware of the harassment their kids suffer. Studies have uncovered a rather large gap between kids' experiences and parents' perception. While at least one-third of students are frustrated by the reality of cyberbullying, a mere 7 percent of parents say they're worried about it affecting their children.

- *Screens create a pressure to be liked* in a world where many females already feel self-conscious about their looks. In fact, some researchers studying this struggle to keep up the perfect image online have observed low self-esteem, loneliness, and deep levels of unhappiness as a direct result of using the web. *A growing number of teenagers use screens for sexting.* Researchers from Drexel University recently surveyed college students, asking them if they had ever sent or received "sexually explicit text messages or images" when they were under age eighteen. Fifty-four percent said yes.

- *Screens provide so many distractions, experts now claim kids shouldn't own them until they are thirteen years old.*

So is this just a bunch of helicopter parents worrying too much, or are some of these legitimate concerns?

Let me come clean.

If I am being completely honest, I'd have to say that a smartphone can be a help or a hindrance. It just depends on who owns whom.

A phone can be a remarkably valuable tool. Let's face it: all the people who wrote those articles mentioned above warning us about the dangers of the overuse of smartphones and social media own smartphones. I own a smartphone. I love it. (I just recently used it to find out the name of the song playing in a restaurant—thanks Shazam!)

So when does tech become a hindrance?

The answer is simple: tech is a great tool, but a lousy crutch. The moment we all become socially dependent on tech. . .Houston, we have a problem.

"Think about it," I challenge teenagers at school assemblies, "how many times have you sat in a circle of your friends and none of them is talking because their heads are all down staring at their phones?"

Students always laugh and point to each other: "That's so you!"

Smartphones can sometimes distract us from the person sitting right in front of us—often a person we care about far more than the endless stream of posts we're scrolling through at the moment.

Don't get me wrong: I believe smartphones can actually help people enhance their personal relationships. Think about how you use it. While eating your breakfast, you can see the new baby pic your best friend posted from a different state. You can text your kids from work to tell them what time you're picking them up. You can call your spouse while driving home. Phones can actually help us connect.

But tech becomes scary when it's our primary source of interpersonal communication. Reason being? Tech actually can hinder normal face-to-face communication.

I've been researching youth culture and technology for decades, and I've encountered countless studies about young people spending too much time with technology. I keep using the word *technology* simply because, if your kids are like mine, then they aren't just staring at their phones, they are also clocking in hours looking at other screens. Even today's video game systems offer interactive and chatting components. All over the country, teens and tweens are sitting in front of TV screens, wearing headsets, and talking with people they've never even met face-to-face as they explore a virtual world together. This may scare parents on many levels, but one by-product of all this screen communication is that the more time young people spend communicating via texting and IM, the less they recognize real-life face-to-face social cues.

For example, in 2014 UCLA did an eye-opening study in which they observed kids who were unplugged and media-free for five days at an outdoor camp. By the end of the five days, these kids were better able to understand emotions and nonverbal cues than kids who were plugged into a normal media diet.

What does this mean? It simply suggests that real-life, face-to-face conversations are superior. Yes, even when we use "emojis"—part of the digital slang of the new millennium—digital communication isn't as powerful as good ol' fashioned face-to-face.

Similarly, researchers witnessed this reality clearly in a bonding experiment in which people engaged in conversation with friends four different ways: in person, and through video chat, audio chat, and instant messaging. As you can probably imagine, bonding was measured and differed "significantly across the conditions." The greatest bonding occurred during the in-person interaction, followed by video chat, audio chat, and then IM, in that order. Good ol' fashioned face-to-face communication always wins.

When today's young people focus on digital connections as their primary social connections, the results are always negative. Research shows that many young people today base their own self-worth and value on online affirmation. The result is too much time trying to impress an online audience and a decline in intimate friendships. In other words, many young people today are substituting true friendships with online "friends."

This even has ramifications in the dating world. A new study by researchers at Stanford and Michigan State found that couples who met online are less likely to stay together long term than those who meet off-line.

So how can parents help teenagers swing the pendulum back toward real-life, face-to-face connections?

Tech Enabled

We need to help teenagers move from being *tech dependent* to *tech enabled*. Phones are really convenient tools for helping us communicate with people *outside the room*, but they become a hindrance when they interfere with our connection with people *inside the room*.

In my "How to Be Smarter Than Your Smartphone" school assembly, after hashing through many of these realities with teens, I always challenge them:

If Mom or Dad accuses you of spending too much time with tech, don't argue. Instead of getting defensive, just prove it with your actions. Slide your phone into your pocket, go hang out with your friends, and talk with them face-to-face. In fact, try this:

- Log off social media for a day and just hang with your friends outside.

- Go on a kayak ride with that girl/guy you talk with so well.

- When you see that beautiful sunset, resist the temptation to snap a pic, find the perfect filter, caption it, and post it on Instagram. Instead, just enjoy the sunset! Maybe even look up and thank the Creator of that beautiful scene. Then pull out your phone and text your mom, telling her when you'll be home.

Tool—yes!

Crutch—nope.

So I ask you, as a parent reading this book, which of these are you modeling?

Our kids will never learn how to be responsible with their phones if we ourselves are slaves to our own devices. It doesn't matter how many lectures we give or how hard we try to teach what we know; we can only reproduce who we are.

I need to hear this just as much as anyone else. As a parent of three, I've failed at this countless times and am regularly learning hard lessons. (I should be brilliant by now, with all the mistakes I've made!) And that's the key: learning from our mistakes, letting them make us better, and then adjusting our behaviors. I call this "adaptive parenting."

As parents, we have the unique opportunity to demonstrate how to use technology responsibly and effectively. As imperfect humans with a phone in our pocket, we can model how to responsibly use our devices for entertainment, for knowledge, and as a tool for connection. More importantly, we can show them how easy it is to actually turn off the TV, set our phone or tablet aside as we enter the dining room, and enjoy a meal together uninterrupted. We can easily keep our phone in our pocket when we're hanging out with friends. We can turn it off when we go away on a three-day camping trip—where we're without a Wi-Fi signal—and actually survive!

This book is full of ideas that may help families look up from their devices and enjoy face-to-face relationships.

Before Diving into This Book

As you read through these fifty-two ideas, you're going to start noticing some common denominators. In fact, some people may be tempted to discount some of them and say, "Eating a family dinner is pretty much the same thing as taking your daughter to coffee!" I'd be quick to reply, "Yes, and taking your kid hunting is really similar to going on a bike ride. They're both outdoor activities that catalyze a climate of continuous conversations." (Nice use of alliteration, huh?) But you'll find these common denominators quite necessary—*and extremely helpful*—for two reasons:

1. **Each of these ideas presents unique characteristics and advice.** In both the "Two-Player Mode" and the "Netflix-Binge Bonding" chapters, you'll notice each setting involves parents actually using technology to connect with their kids. Similarly, you may notice several chapters helping you use questions to engage kids in conversation ("Fingertip Questions," "The *My Big Fat Greek Wedding* Method," et al.). Each of these chapters will provide new tools you can use for these specific situations. Besides. . .

2. **Your kids' tastes are going to vary.** One kid may really respond to late-night splurges but may never be interested in stopping for frozen yogurt on the way home from school. Another may be open to no tech at the table but would freak out at the mere suggestion of a media fast, especially regimented No-Tech Tuesdays. If your kids are like mine, they'll be unique in taste and temperament. The more ideas you have in your arsenal, the better.

So enjoy these ideas, most of which I've drawn not only from years of research, but from my years out on the front lines as an imperfect parent who wanted to connect with his kids. These are many ideas that worked for my wife and me. I hope some of them will be a help for you as well.

The Coviewing
Connection

Way back in 2004, I read about a California mom who learned the hard way that she didn't know as much about her kid as she thought she did.

Roberta "Bobbi" MacKinnon died from injuries after being flung from a playground merry-go-round propelled by a rope tied to the back of a vehicle. Bobbi and her friends had watched the MTV show Jackass and decided to try to copy their merry-go-round stunt. The result was fatal.

I read about the story in my local newspaper. Joan MacKinnon, Bobbi's mother, said, "I had no idea that she watched the show. Maybe I would have made her stop and think that this is dangerous fun."

I clearly remember my reaction reading Bobbi's mother's words that day. I swallowed hard and thought, That could be me! I don't know every show my kids watch.

In the silence of the moment, I heard the TV on in the other room. I thought, Oh great! My kids are watching something right now, and I don't even know what it is!

I popped up from my chair and ran into the other room. They were watching the cartoon *SpongeBob SquarePants*.

As I stood there in the doorway, I recalled a study I had just read in the journal *Pediatrics,* revealing the importance of parental guidelines with entertainment media. One of the techniques the authors suggested was "coviewing"—simply sitting down and watching entertainment media with your children so you can use it as an opportunity to talk about important family values.

So I sat down and watched *SpongeBob* with my kids (and found it quite hilarious. . .especially that Patrick!).

In a world where we are constantly at battle with kids and their screens, coviewing can be a really fun practice where you join them enjoying screen time. After all, we're talking about a lot of screen time per day.

The screen today's teenagers stare at more than any other is that small one they carry around with them in their pocket. In fact, according to the Common Sense Media report I cited at the beginning of this book, teens spend two hours, forty-two minutes per day on their smartphones alone, then one hour, thirty-seven minutes on a computer, and another one hour, thirty-one minutes watching TV. That's just the "average kid." So your own kids may spend more or less time on these devices. And you can be sure that if your daughter doesn't watch ninety-one minutes of TV per day, she has a friend at school who is more than making up for it in her home.

The point I'm making is this: use some of this screen time as a point of connection.

No, coviewing is not the most social activity you can do as a parent, but it accomplishes two tasks:

1. ***It gives you a peek into their world of entertainment media.*** What shows do your kids watch? What online videos do they frequent? What is the content of all this entertainment? What lessons are they walking away with after watching it? Many parents have no idea what kind of entertainment their kids are consuming on their screens. Do you?

2. ***It provides you with a springboard for conversations about what you just watched.*** When a major character makes a decision, simply ask your kids a question when the show is over. "Was he right?" Sometimes

that simple three-word question can spark a debate between siblings where all you need to do is sit back and eat popcorn while they do all the talking. Other times it may necessitate asking more questions to provoke further discussion. Don't feel the need to discuss everything you watch. This will quickly grow tiresome. But don't hesitate to jump on occasional opportunities.

Coviewing opens up a host of possibilities for conversation. No, I'm not endorsing watching just anything with your kids. If you begin watching something with your kids and it is completely against your family values, then it's your job as a parent to say, "Sorry, kids, we aren't going to watch this." Or, better yet, ask them, "Kids, do you think we should watch this? Why not?"

Avoid overreaction. If you freak out every time you sit down to watch something with your kids, they're going to hide from you and only watch TV at their friends' houses. Make these coviewing connections a pleasant experience. Discover fun shows that you all enjoy watching together.

By the way, coviewing can be done on any size screen, not just on the fifty-five-incher in your living room (more on that later).

So look for those opportunities to simply enjoy some entertainment together. This practice can provide fun bonding times and sometimes a good springboard for conversation.

Looking for some questions to ask your kids in this setting? Remember to turn to the back of this book where you'll find a chapter summary and sample questions to ask your kids for each of these 52 chapters.

Questions to ponder:

- Do you know what your kids watch on their devices, on the computer, or on TV?

- When is a good time for you to plop down next to your kids and "coview" with them?

- What are some examples of content you won't allow to be seen in your house?

- How will you address objectionable content without "freaking out"?

- What is an example of a show your kids like that you can enjoy with them?

The Fine Art of Shutting Up

My oldest kid would be the first to tell you, "Dad loves to lecture." The problem is, the more I talked, the less my kids listened. It probably took me until my third kid before I finally got the hint: *dialogue is far more effective than monologue.*

Dialogue = a conversation. Both parties engaged.

Monologue = a lecture. One party dozing while the other rattles on and on.

One of the best parenting practices I've been implementing recently is simply shutting up and listening. Think about it. It's hard for us to expect others to talk to us when we're doing all the talking. If you really want to connect with your kids, the first step may be slapping a giant piece of duct tape across your own mouth.

Try it. It's amazing what you can learn when you just sit back like a fly on the wall, observing your kids and listening. Try this when you drive a car full of your kids' friends. Shut up, and they'll forget you're there. You'll learn many things about your son or daughter's world that you didn't know before.

Better yet, if you want to get your teenager talking, try this at the dinner table: put your own phone or tablet aside, ask a question, then resist the urge to talk.

It may take a few questions to prime the pump. My youngest never answers the first question I ask. I have to toss a few questions out there and wait it out like a fisherman.

Eventually she'll kill the silence.

The same thing happens on my daddy-daughter dates. At first, my girls tend to be quiet. In my early years as a parent, I made the mistake of filling dead air with my voice. I'd talk and talk and talk. . . .

Before I knew it, the entire night was finished and my daughters had said three words.

Not much fun for them.

Think about this for a moment. Most parents would love for their kids to set their phones or tablets aside, look up at us, and engage in meaningful dialogue. This sounds like a dream come true. The sobering question we may want to ask ourselves is, do we even give them this opportunity? Do our kids feel like they have a parent who would listen?

A youth worker I know recently polled her middle school and high school students, asking them to write down advice for their parents. I posted the responses on my blog (JonathanMcKeeWrites.com). The most common pieces of advice kids wrote down were "Hear what I have to say" and "Listen to me!"

Others wrote, "Talk with me more," "Respect me," and "Be more understanding."

Guess what? This isn't bad news. This just means that our kids want to be noticed and heard. (Maybe that's why they're spending so much time on social networks.)

Do your kids feel noticed and heard?

I've slowly been learning to shut up. Not dead silence—I just ask a few questions and then play the quiet one. Allow me to emphasize the word *few*. This isn't a chance for us to inundate them with irritating questions:

How was school?
Did you have any tests? How did you do?
Do you have any homework? Then do it!!!

Are you their parole officer or their parent?

If you really want to engage your kids in conversation, put some thought and creativity into your questions:

If school were canceled tomorrow and you could go anywhere for the day, where would you go?

Who would you want to bring with you?

What is it that you enjoy so much about this friend?

Questions like this unveil your kids' dreams, their favorite activities, and their favorite people to hang out with. Wouldn't that be good to know?

Provide your kids a listening ear. Make an effort to engage them in meaningful dialogue. Resist the urge to monologue.

Do you know how your kids would answer if you asked these questions?

What are you waiting for?

Questions to ponder:

- Which is your tendency, dialogue or monologue?

- Why do you think dialogue is more effective than monologue?

- What are some questions that may provoke conversation with your kids? (I'll devote the entire next chapter to coming up with questions on the fly.)

3 Fingertip Questions

We're only a few chapters into the book, and I've already encouraged you repeatedly to use questions as a tool to engage your kids. Maybe you're already wondering, *Jonathan, how can we come up with these questions on the fly?*

Sadly, I never think of the perfect question until about three hours after the conversation, when I look back in retrospect and conclude, "I probably should have said. . ."

So what do you do in these moments? After all, this book is really about connecting with your kid, not correcting or disciplining your kid.

Maybe you've watched Netflix with your teenagers, and you can't help but notice one of the main characters in the show constantly engaging in irresponsible behaviors—with no consequences whatsoever.

You remember one of the most important principles in parenting today: Don't freak out. You don't want to overreact to the situation, cementing in your kids' minds, I had better never share any of my struggles with Dad because this is how he'll respond.

One step better, remember to replace lecturing with listening. This is where you ask a well-placed question to help your kids think through the ramifications of their choices.

The problem is you have no idea what to ask.

Maybe your kids tell you a story about a friend at school who is spreading rumors about another student. Is this one of those teaching moments? If only you could ask them questions that would help them think through their values and behaviors.

The world provides us plenty of teaching moments each day. It's our job as parents to use them every once in a while (I say every "once in a while" because our kids would quickly tire of discussion time every time they play their music). The key to springboarding these good discussions is well-placed questions. Sure, you can always collect creative questions from books (like the bonus questions I provide for each chapter at the end of this book, or my book *Get Your Teenager Talking*, which provides more than one thousand questions to ask). But what about those times when we don't have time to refer to a book?

Here are four quick, practical tips to help you ask well-placed questions on the fly. We'll use the example of driving with your teens, and they plug their phone into the car to listen to their favorite playlist. Note: Our kids are never going to be excited when we inquire about their entertainment choices. We're messing with something they cherish greatly. But questions are a far better approach than lecturing. The following tips are just a rough outline of how you could approach the conversation. You probably wouldn't ask all the questions, and you definitely wouldn't ask them so formally. The point is to give your kids a chance to share their opinions without interruption.

1. *Observation*

The first step to helping our kids think through situations is getting them to pause for a moment and simply observe what they just encountered. This can be achieved by merely asking, "What did she just say?"

This simple question nudges young people to stop and take notice of the image they just saw or the lyrics they're bathing in every day.

2. Interpretation

The next natural question is "What does she mean?"

Yes. Play dumb.

Basically, that makes our kids actually process the content—maybe even for the first time. This question subtly hints, *lyrics matter*. We're not merely shrugging our shoulders and saying, "Who cares?" We're taking notice. Sometimes our kids aren't really even paying attention to the lyrics. Sure, they may *hear* them. They may even be able to sing them back to you word for word. But they've never *processed* the lyrics and *pondered* them.

So innocently ask, "What does she mean?"

These questions lead to the next natural step. . . .

3. Opinion

Ask your kids for their two cents. Ask:

"How's that going to work out for her?"

"Has she thought this through?"

"What's right?"

These questions provoke our kids to offer insight based on their own personal values. Instead of telling our kids how to think, we are asking them what they think. And as they're stumbling through their own values, ask them one last question to steer them toward truth.

4. Foundation

Direct your kids toward your family values. If your relationship with God is important to you, then you may want to ask, "What does the Bible say about this?"

If your kids don't know the exact chapter and verse, be ready to direct them. Yes, this requires you to be in God's Word yourself so you know where to point. Don't worry; if you don't know a scripture offhand, don't be afraid to admit it and then suggest, "Let's look this one up later when we get home."

Again, you might not ask all of these questions. Your conversation may only require one simple question: "Is he right?" That question alone is powerful. Don't turn every TV show or car ride into a teaching moment. Less is more.

Well-placed questions open doors to meaningful conversations. If you're like me—prone to lecture—questions help you replace monologue with dialogue.

Questions to ponder:

- Can you think of a time when a thoughtful question sparked a conversation with your kid?

- Can you think of a moment in the last week when you could have paused and asked your kids a question?

- How do you think your kids would have responded to those questions?

- Could this discussion have led to dialogue about any of your family values?

The Teen Genius Bar

What do you do when you can't figure out an app on your phone?

If you're like me, you just give it to one of your teenagers.

"Alyssa, how do you block this idiot who just spammed my Facebook timeline?" went one of my many questions to my daughter.

Today's parents are raising a generation who seemingly came out of the womb clutching a cell phone. They've been using technology since before they spoke their first word, and they have a knack for it. By the time they're teens, many of them are walking, talking Genius Bars.

Use this as a point of interaction.

Young people love being the expert. Add to that the fact that most adults ignore young people; when you give a young person attention and respect, it will usually be reciprocated.

So if you can't figure out your TV, computer, or phone, ask your kids for help. If it's in their knowledge set, they'll usually be glad to show you how to do it.

This can usually be followed by some natural follow-up questions. If they help you tweak your social media profile, ask them questions that flow from the conversation:

- What's your favorite app?
- What do you do when people frustrate you on these apps?
- What do you do when you stumble across inappropriate material?

Be careful. Don't ask these questions like a parole officer looking for malfeasance. Ask with a genuine tone of curiosity. Think of the conversation as a bonding experience, not a teaching moment. Sure, as you can see from the questions I just asked, sometimes teaching moments will naturally pop up. Use them, but don't force them. Just ask your kids' honest opinion and then listen. Remember, the idea is to make them feel valued for their opinion or expertise.

If you ever buy a new piece of technology, you may not even have to ask for your kids' help. They'll come to you!

Way back when the PlayStation 3 (PS3) came out, it was one of the first Blu-ray disc players. I'm a movie fanatic and had been looking forward to Blu-ray technology for years (1080p resolution compared to the inferior DVD!). When the PS3 was released, Blu-ray players sold for about $1,000. The PS3 was only $699.

So I bought a PS3—to watch movies!

I stood in line at Best Buy and got one of the first ones.

My son came home from school and saw me playing old-school games on the PS3. He just about did a backflip!

"Yeah! We got a PS3!"

None of his friends had one. But his cool dad did!

So I told him, "This is my Blu-ray player. But, yes, if you'd like to play games on it, feel free."

The two of us began navigating the world of PS3, downloading some old-school games (I downloaded Qbert) and figuring out the network settings. We did this as a team. I treated him like an equal throughout the process.

"What's this?" I'd ask.

"Oh, that's the way you can connect with other gamers!" he eagerly replied.

I never had to pry any conversation out of Alec where the PS3 was concerned. I had his full attention. And more importantly, he had mine.

Give your kids opportunities to be the expert and show you how to do something. You'll both benefit from this bonding time.

Questions to ponder:

- What technology do your kids love the most?

- What areas of social media or technology might your kids be able to advise you about?

- How can you approach the subject with them?

"No phones in the bedroom, especially at night."

It's a practice countless doctors and parenting experts recommend, but I'm warning you: your kids will absolutely hate it.

It's not a popular notion, but it's one I happen to believe. Teens and tweens, especially young ones, shouldn't have their phones in their bedrooms at night. So I recommend that Mom and Dad tell their kids, "We'll charge your phones each night in our bedroom."

Joke with them, if you will: "It's a free service we provide as your parents. No fees applied."

Here's the problem: if you didn't start this practice when your kids were young, then expect World War III. I'm just shooting straight with you. After years of talking to teenagers about this at events and school assemblies, I recognize this subject gets teenagers heated.

Why?

They don't know any different.

Most teens are allowed to have their phones and devices in their bedrooms. I talk with parents consistently about this at my parenting workshops, and it's obvious to me that most of them don't enforce boundaries in this area. Even if they do have boundaries, the majority of their kids' friends probably don't. Additionally, if your kids have been watching the Disney Channel for years, they've probably gleaned that most parents are idiots and should let their kids do whatever they want.

But healthy parenting involves both bonding and

boundaries. Both elements are key. Even though this book is primarily focused on bonding, boundaries can actually help create the arena where good bonding can exist.

Think of it like basketball. When a group of kids play basketball, they don't necessarily think of rules as helpful, but if one kid decided to punch people in the face and take the ball away, then those rules would become way more necessary. In fact, the rules would actually make the game more fun (otherwise, the NBA becomes UFC).

Boundaries are necessary in life as well. And this is one of the times in this book when I'll recommend laying down some boundaries, because they are crucial if you want to make sure phones and other technologies don't become unhealthy distractions.

But brace yourselves. If you advise your kids to charge their phones in a family docking station in your bedroom at night, they are likely to freak out. This won't be an easy battle.

When I first talked with my kids about no phones in the bedroom at night, they rolled their eyes at me and said, "Dad, all my friends have their phones in their bedrooms!" Then their arguments became a little more strategic: "But Dad, I need it to wake me up in the morning."

I kindly let them know about this really cool invention known as an alarm clock.

But that wasn't enough to convince them. I had to give them more.

Allow me to give you the facts so you can be equipped for this conversation:

In 2010 the American Academy of Pediatrics (AAP) advised parents to remove televisions and computers from their children's bedrooms. Some parents listened. Most didn't.

But then everything changed. In 2012 America passed the 50 percent mark in smartphone ownership. Now more than half of Americans had Internet access on their phones, which were now both computers and TVs in one mobile platform.

Smartphone penetration expanded rapidly. By 2015 more than 75 percent of American twelve- to seventeen-year-olds owned smartphones. Now, as you read this, the majority of young people carry around a mobile device with access to TV, movies, music, social media, Google, and YouTube—all the stuff the AAP advised parents to remove from the bedroom. And the AAP didn't amend its stance; in fact, they still recommend, "Keep the TV set and Internet-connected electronic devices out of the child's bedroom."

How many parents do you know who stand outside their kids' bedrooms saying, "Please deposit your phone in this bucket"?

Do you do this?

The majority of kids have smartphones in their bedrooms all night long. And according to the most recent National Sleep Foundation report, which I cited at the beginning of this book, the majority of young people leave these devices on. Sadly, those who leave their phone on, average almost an hour less sleep than those who either turn off their phones or don't have them in their rooms.

So what's the answer for today's parents?

If your kids are young—listen to the AAP and set precedent early. Buy a family docking station where you charge all devices at night. Place this docking station in your bedroom so your kids are not tempted to sneak and access their devices in the middle of the night.

If your daughter is already seventeen and leaving for college in six months, it's probably not worth the nuclear holocaust that will happen if you try to take her phone away at night. Instead, engage in dialogue with her about her phone use. Interact with her in discussions like the ones I address in the upcoming "Elephant in the Room" chapter of this book. Share reports like the ones I cited in the intro chapter and ask her what she thinks. Help her think through being smarter than her smartphone.

What if your son is fourteen or fifteen and has already had his phone in his room for several years? I advise you to begin engaging in discussions with him, warning him that you are favoring the family docking station. Allow him to vent a little and plead his case. Hear him out. Think about it or even pray about it with him for a week. He may come to understand that all these experts value his well-being over his convenience. Don't be afraid to lovingly enforce boundaries that protect your kids.

The family docking station isn't a prison camp, and it's not grounding your kids from their devices. It's an eight- or nine-hour break from technology to get needed rest. It's yet another discipline that helps your kids realize they can survive without their phones by their side.

Their phones aren't the only things that need a recharge each day. Help them take a break from entertainment media and tech each night.

Questions to ponder:

- Why do you think the AAP and other parenting experts advise no screens in young people's bedrooms?

- Do your kids have computers or TVs in their bedrooms?

- Where do your kids keep their mobile devices at night? How's that working for them?

- How will your kids respond if you decide to use a family docking station? How could you implement this with the least resistance?

6 The Value of Noticing

How many times have you been grocery shopping or in a restaurant and you see a mom or dad chatting on the phone *and totally ignoring their kid?*

How many times have you been that parent?

Yeah, me too.

It's sad. . .but if we're being honest, it happens. Sometimes we make the vital mistake of letting our own world overwhelm us to the point that we ignore our kids. This hurts us in two ways:

1. Our actions communicate loud and clear where our priorities are (more on this later when I encourage parents to "put the phone down!")

2. We miss out on the awesome opportunity to simply pause and take in everything there is to know about our kids through simple observation.

Let's not make this more difficult than it is. Connecting with our kids starts with the simple act of "noticing."

Have you noticed. . .

*   who is your kid's best friend?

*   who texts him or her the most?

*   what social media do they use the most?

*   what do they order at Starbucks?

*   what store would be your kid's first stop if he or she had $100 to spend?

- what songs are on your kid's favorite playlist? What do they call the playlist?
- who your kid would call if they needed someone who would really listen?

Dads, moms—how much do you really know about your kids? And how hard would it be to make some of these observations?

I'll be transparent here: I've failed to do this more times than I can count. For example, one time my daughter came home from school, greeted me quickly, and then went quietly to her room. I was busy, so I didn't pay it much mind. Later that evening, my dad called me and asked, "What's wrong with Alyssa?"

I didn't have any idea what he was talking about. "What do you mean?" I asked him.

"She's been posting some pretty depressing stuff."

I grabbed my phone and clicked on her favorite place to post. There it was, clear for everyone to see—and I missed it. But my seventy-year-old dad hadn't. (And I teach parents how to do this stuff!) I went upstairs, knocked on Alyssa's door, and then sat next to her in her room. After a little bit of listening, I realized I really had missed some clear signs that she was having a bad week.

No, I'm not asking you to spy on your kids. I'm asking you just to lift your eyes from your newspaper, your phone, your TV show, or your mail and just *notice* the following:

- Where do your kids hang out the most?
- What do they do there?
- Who are they with?
- Where do they spend time online?

- What do they post?
- Who do they connect with in their cyberworld?
- What do they like to wear?
- What do their clothes tell you about their self-esteem, their personal taste, and their hygiene?
- What angers them? What breaks their hearts?
- What excites them? What are they passionate about?

This book repeatedly points out how teenagers struggle to look up from their devices. But let's be honest. Many parents have the same struggle, and, consequently, the chasm between parent and child only grows.

My suggestion is simple: look up from your phone when your kids are around. Better yet, put away your technology and *notice* them.

The more we learn about our kids, the better we can connect with them. If we know their favorite place to eat, shop, or hang out, then we have a good chance of connecting with them at those places. Similarly, if we know their likes, their fears, and their passions, we can use those as points of connection and conversation.

But it all starts with just *noticing*.

What is your kid doing right now?

Questions to ponder:

- What distracts you from noticing your kids?

- Which of the above observations have you already noticed?

- Which are some you have *not* noticed?

- How could you use some of these observations to better connect with your kids?

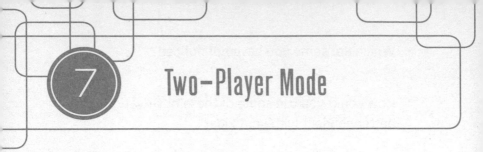

7 Two-Player Mode

"Dad, you wanna play Xbox?"

This is one of those moments when parents sometimes just need to say, "Yes." Who cares if you are in the middle of organizing your garage or going through the mail? Set it aside! Two-player mode is by far one of the most effective ways to connect with a generation of young people who love screens.

Sadly, I passed up so many good opportunities to bond with my son this way, and I regret each and every one of them.

I had multiple reasons why I said, "No" or "Not now":

- *I was busy.* We all could make this excuse. Yet U.S. adults average four and a half hours per day watching TV (that's more than our teens). So it's really not that we don't have time, it's that we choose some other recreational activity, be it TV, golf, or working in the garage.

- *I was lousy at Xbox.* Don't get me wrong—I'm not lousy at video games. I'm just not wired for these newer controllers with more buttons than I have fingers. When I was a kid, the Atari joystick had one button and a stick. That was all I needed to blow away asteroids all night long! Now controllers are like the cockpit of an airplane. I stink at Xbox.

- *I preferred outdoor activities.* I'd choose hiking up a mountain or paddling down a river any day over navigating some virtual world, as fun as that may be. Plus, all technology is bad. . .right?

What's your excuse?

Video games provide a fantastic opportunity to bond with our kids. In fact, video games are far better than watching TV or movies, because video games are conducive to dialoguing while you play.

Today's young people, especially boys, love video games. A recent Common Sense Media study found that "teen boys average 56 minutes a day playing video games, compared with only seven minutes for girls." Have you tried to connect with your boys during this time?

Personally, I found my son to be extremely engaging during video game time compared with other activities. Five minutes into playing two-player mode in his favorite game, he would start asking me questions. I didn't even have to initiate conversation.

For him, I think it was the fact that I was investing time in something he truly enjoyed. The bonding we experienced created a climate where conversation was cultivated. And sometimes conversation flows easier when two people are doing a task side by side.

If your kids never ask you to play, don't worry. Just walk in the room sometime when they are playing. Make sure you display a posture of sheer curiosity and interest, not judgment. Ask occasional questions if they are silent, questions like, "Who is that guy?" Use compliments hidden within the question: "How did you get that cool sword?"

Before you know it, you may hear the words you're looking for: "Do you want to try?"

Does this mean you have to spend five hours playing video games with your kid every day after school? Not at all. Play for thirty minutes and then say, "Oh man, I wish I could play more, but I gotta finish our taxes." Without lecturing, you're subtly exemplifying self-imposed media guardrails.

But most importantly, just have fun playing games with

your kids. Two-player mode is an amazing tool for connection. Try it. You may enjoy it more than you expect.

Questions to ponder:

- Did you enjoy video games when you were a kid? Why or why not?

- Why do you think kids open up during "two-player" mode?

- Which of your kids might respond to this kind of bonding time?

8

The Late–Night Splurge Sensation

It's Thursday night, already past bedtime, and the kids have had a busy week. Instead of your routine "Off to bed with ya!" Try something else, something like this: "Who's up for ordering pizza?"

Is this extremely unhealthy?

Certainly.

Something you should do every Thursday night?

Definitely not.

But a fun memory your kids will never forget?

Absolutely.

Life is full of disciplines and routine. Every once in a while, it's fun to break with that routine, jump at the chance to splurge, and build a significant memory. And I don't know many teenagers (especially teenage boys) who wouldn't jump at the chance to stay up and indulge in something delicious.

If your kids don't like pizza, make it a late-night sundae or some other treat you know they'll like. The point is, break the monotony of the typical Thursday night and provide an opportunity just to hang out.

If your kids are like mine, their phone is often right by their side. In this situation, I'd make it just like any other family meal—no tech. In our house, we don't bring our phones to the table. The table is a tech-free zone (more on that later in this book). If their tendency would be to bring their phone, you may even have to verbalize a disclaimer when you offer the pizza: "You guys could go to bed right now, or if you go put your phones away in their chargers, you can come back down and I'll order some pizza and wings!"

Be proactive about creating an atmosphere of fun, uninterrupted conversation.

If your kids aren't used to this kind of conversation, then use one of the tools you've already read about in this book to spark some fun dialogue: creative questions. One of the first questions in my book *Get Your Teenagers Talking* always seems to work:

- "If you could text anyone in the world and you know they'd text you back, who would you text?"

Then follow that up with more questions:

- "What would you text that person?"
- "What would you hope that person texts you back?"

My kids always like it when we splurge and let them stay up late. Thursdays are a good night to spring this occasionally because they have only one school day left and you won't mess them up for the whole week.

Questions to ponder:

- What food would your kids definitely stay up for?

- What are some examples of spontaneous splurges you've done like this?

- Why do you think that food is a good catalyst to conversation?

9 Addressing the Elephant. . .er. . . the Smartphone in the Room

This book is packed with ideas for connection and fun conversation with your kids. But what happens when parents feel the need to address the elephant in the room—the kid who won't look up from his/her smartphone?

I've seen polarized responses to this question. On one extreme, we have the parent who is constantly "up in the kid's business." This parent has downloaded every piece of software in existence to track her or his kids, monitor their every thumbstroke, and quiz them the second they walk in the door.

"Who is this Chris you were texting at 1:37 this afternoon?" comes the accusatory question when the teen walks in the door.

Sadly, kids of a parent like this one often count the days until they turn eighteen and escape the prison camp.

On the other extreme, we have the parent who just hands the kid a smartphone and delivers the only instructions the kid will ever receive: "Don't break it."

These kids never learn anything about media discernment and responsibility. They learn by trial and error, often paying a high price for some of those errors.

Don't feel the need to float toward either extreme. It's okay to provide helpful boundaries and to incrementally lessen those guardrails on your kids' road to independence. In other words, you might start strict, with lots of guidance, but as your kids grow and mature, you can slowly provide them the freedom to make some of these decisions on their own while still under your shadow.

Exactly how strict or lenient should parents be? That's the one question that still draws debate from experts. But when the smoke clears from this debate, *every*—and I truly mean every—expert agrees on one common denominator: frequent conversations.

So what does this look like?

Take what you've learned so far in this book (notice, affirm, ask questions. . .shut up) and engage your kids in dialogue *about their phones*. If you notice their phone distracting them from people in the room, address it creatively. Don't confront them. Just bring up the issue and ask for their opinion. Share an article, like the many I mentioned in the introduction of this book, and ask them questions.

Consider the 2014 UCLA study I noted at the beginning of this book, observing kids who were unplugged and media-free for five days at an outdoor camp. Ask your kids, "Why were these kids better able to understand emotions and nonverbal cues after five days than kids who were plugged into a normal media diet?"

It's always shrewd to ask questions about other kids first, instead of directing questions right at your own kids. In other words, don't ask your kids, "Have you noticed that the smartphone is numbing your brain and turning you into an imbecile?" Instead, start with general questions, and then slowly segue toward questions about their world.

Here's a sample of what this discussion may look like with a progression of questions. Read a summary paragraph from an article or study, and then follow up with some simple questions, like this:

Take a peek at this bonding experiment where people engaged in conversation with friends four different ways: in person, video chat, audio chat, and instant messaging. Researchers watched people communicate all these different ways and then measured the outcome. The results differed "significantly across the conditions."

1. Can you guess which communication method helped people bond the most?
2. The greatest bonding occurred during the in-person interaction, followed by video chat, audio chat, and then IM, in that order. Why do you think this was the case?
3. Why is communication more effective when people can see facial expressions?
4. Do you ever notice a group of young people hanging out together, and all of them have their heads down looking at their phone? Why is this?
5. Why do you think people sometimes ignore the people in the room?
6. How can people better maximize face-to-face communication?
7. What might this look like in your world?

(Notice that I didn't really ask a pointed question until the last query.)

Note: These questions are just a rough outline of what you could ask. You probably shouldn't ask them all, and you most definitely don't want to sound like a scientist, or worse, an interrogator when you ask them. So make the questions flow naturally, keeping the conversation simple and age appropriate.

Don't be afraid to use teaching moments. Keep your eyes open for articles and studies and ask your kids their opinion. Share the AAP report from the "Family Docking Station" chapter, in which doctors recommended no phones in kids' bedrooms. Ask your kids, "Why do you think doctors recommend this?" Make it a dialogue, not a monologue. Do far more listening than lecturing.

Subscribe to free articles like those I provide on TheSource4Parents.com. I link more studies on that web page than you could ever discuss. Then apply some of the fingertip questions I presented in chapter 3.

When the overuse of (dare I say "addiction to") technology becomes a problem in your home (and it probably will), don't be afraid to address it in this kind of calm, calculated, and creative manner.

Questions to ponder:

- What unhealthy use of technology may need to be addressed at your house?

- How can you address it?

- What are some articles or studies you may be able to reference?

- What are some questions you can ask to help your kids open up about this issue?

10 The House to "Hang"

"Dad, can Megan spend the night. . .*on a school night*?"
  "Absolutely."
  "Can we feed her dinner?"
  "Unquestionably."

  "This Sunday night, we're all thinking of going somewhere to watch movies."
  "Pack 'em in our family room. That's why we bought that big sectional."

  "Mom, my group from history class has to work on our presentation for tomorrow. We need a place to meet. Can we—"
  "Say no more. Bring them all over here. I'll buy pizza and Mexican sodas." (Italy and Mexico get along well in our house.)

  This year has provided plenty of opportunities for hospitality—*costly* opportunities.
  As I began writing this book last year my youngest daughter was a senior in high school with a driver's license and countless friends to hang out with. The question is simple: Would I rather my daughter hang out at someone else's house or have her here at home?
  Don't get me wrong; we don't have her chained to her bedroom. She hangs out at friends' houses often. We just make sure our house is always a welcoming option. This year we've not only committed time but also money to this practice.
  Providing the house to "hang" reaps all kinds of rewards:

1. **First, it provides a social home for my daughter and her friends.** When my daughter has her friends over, they hang out in our family room connected to the kitchen. This is the most social room in the house, so we get to meet all her friends and engage them in conversation. The more I get to know my daughter's friends, the more she opens up to me about them, because I'm "in the loop."

2. **Second, kids don't defer to their phones even half as often in a house overflowing with face-to-face conversations.** Young people are social creatures. The more we put them in a room full of their peers, the more they socially interact. Does this mean they never look at their phones if friends are in the room? Sadly, no. I've walked in a room full of teenagers countless times and found them all staring at their own phones (and promptly start teasing them for doing it, which usually gets them talking, pleading their case about how much they are not addicted).

3. **Third, it just makes me feel good knowing where my daughter is and who she's with.**

Seize the opportunity to have your kids' friends over for dinner. Sure, this can be a budget item, but it doesn't have to be a big one. If you can't afford pizza and soft drinks, then make a big pot of spaghetti and put out a pitcher of lemonade. Any money spent is well worth it. This isn't bribery, this is just shrewd parenting. Food tends to catalyze conversation. Kids are less inclined to bury their heads in their phones when they are stuffing their faces. Some of my best conversations with my kids and their friends were over dinner.

We need to be proactive as parents to demonstrate the "house to hang" hospitality loud and clear. One of my blog readers, Scott, shared how he and his wife created a policy in their house called "The Chips Are for Nothing." The idea was that certain foods are often designated for certain recipes or certain meals and are deemed "off limits." Kids are therefore scared to eat snacks because they don't want to get into trouble. So Scott's family declared, "The chips are for nothing." In other words, when friends are over, chips are always open game. You needn't ask. Even if they had been bought for Taco Tuesday or something special, the grocery store always has more.

Our kids will be way more inclined to invite friends over if we create a climate that is welcoming in all aspects.

Providing a house to hang out also provides opportunities to mentor your kids' friends. My wife and I became go-to people for many of my kids' friends. It wasn't uncommon for one of my daughters to ask Lori, "Mom, can you talk with Tiffani? She needs some advice." Their friends had talked with her at our house and they knew Lori was "safe."

This all starts with simple hospitality.

Are you providing a place where conversation is encouraged?

Questions to ponder:

- Why do you think people tend to open up and talk while eating?

- Where do your kids like to hang out? Why?

- What could you do to make your house more hospitable?

11 The Media–Fast Fulfillment

We happened upon this little practice when my two oldest kids, both in high school at the time, decided to go on a missions trip. The trip required some rigorous training, including a "fast." This was no ordinary fast. The leader challenged the kids to give up media and technology.

Shouldn't be a big deal, right?

Wrong. We're talking about the lifeblood of today's teen and tween. Remember what I shared in the introduction to this book: recent studies reveal that teens spend almost nine hours a day soaking in media and technology (eight hours, fifty-six minutes to be exact). Tweens, kids ages eight through twelve, spend six hours (exactly five hours, fifty-five minutes). With that in mind, consider what a media fast requires of a teenager.

Sound crazy? Well, it gets crazier. The leader of this trip challenged our kids to give up all entertainment media and technology for *an entire month*.

Yeah! Kids were freaking out. Many reconsidered whether they even wanted to go on the trip.

Then this leader took it one step further: he challenged all the kids' parents to do the same thing.

I wasn't excited about it, but our family went for it.

At first, we were all whining. No Internet (other than for homework or work required by school), no texting, no music, no movies—*nothing*. It was amazing how quiet it was around the house.

As Yoda says, we had to "unlearn what we had learned." I'd get in the car and turn on the music. My kids would say, "Dad! No music."

They had to remind me!

But then something began happening.

Talking!

Lots of talking (there was nothing else to do).

Each night, we'd break out a deck of cards or a board game, or head out on a walk around the neighborhood. It was fun. It was like camping, but in our own house. It was like living out a zombie apocalypse. . .except with no dead people walking around.

We dialogued more that month than we had in the six months prior.

The experience was life changing. One month of hanging out as a family around the fireplace, reading, playing games, laughing—it was truly amazing.

Am I recommending that you force your family to fast from entertainment media and technology for a month? Not at all. Your suggestion would probably be met with laughter, followed by a brief silence, then, "Wait. . .you were serious?"

The media fast we tried was an amazing experience, but it was one that the teenagers owned and that had the momentum and support of the entire youth group. More than seventy teenagers did it together, and they still complained.

But it became an impactful experience for all.

It's been interesting to see people get a taste of this, in much smaller doses, across the world. I've read countless articles of families, schools, and even businesses that declared a "tech-free" day to cleanse their digital palate. Some have tried several days or a week, and I always hear the same results: "It was difficult at first, but the experience was eye opening."

Why not give it a try? Google this: "teens media fast no smartphone for a day" and then click around at the articles you discover. Then, at dinner one night, engage your kids in a discussion like the one outlined in chapter 9, "Addressing the. . .Smartphone in the Room," where you ask them about an article and get them to share their thoughts. But this time, also read a little about a media fast and ask, "What do you think? Is this a good idea for some kids to try?" (Again, start with a question about kids in general.)

Then don't be afraid to challenge them: "Do you think you guys could go an entire day without entertainment media or technology?"

Don't expect your kids to jump on board immediately. This may take several conversations and time for the principle to really sink in. But then try it. Make it happen for a day, or maybe even a couple days. See what happens.

It may be one of the best things your kids ever experience.

For our family and our church, the experience was truly life changing. So much so that when the fast was over, we actually missed it.

And that's when we began the next practice I want to share with you (you'll have to turn the page to see that one).

Questions to ponder:

- How would your kids respond if they were challenged to fast from media and technology for a day? For a week? For a month?

- What about you? How would you respond?

- If, hypothetically, you tried it. . .what would it look like in your home?

- What's stopping you from trying it for a day?

12 The No-Tech Tuesday Tactic

After our family went one month without entertainment media and technology, we were damaged goods. That fast made a sizable dent in our lives.

We couldn't revert back to media slavery.

So we decided to bring it back. Not for a month (no way— that was too difficult), but for one night a week.

That was the beginning of "No-Tech Tuesdays."

No-Tech Tuesdays didn't start until after school on Tuesday afternoons. It was, more accurately, No-Tech Tuesday afternoons and evenings. It was one evening a week with no TV, no Internet, no texting, no music—*nothing*.

It was fantastic.

Funny, when our kids would have friends over on a Tuesday, they would tell them, "Oh, it's No-Tech Tuesday."

It was always fun to see their friends' faces.

No-Tech. . .what?

Once our kids' friends tried it, they got a taste of the good life: conversation, board games, reading, throwing the ball for the dog outside until he'd eventually tire. They would often say, "I wish my family would try this!"

It was interesting how this dynamic evolved as my kids grew older. For example, when my two oldest kids were off at college and my youngest was playing "only child" for two years, we'd often shoot the older kids a picture of the three of us chilling in the family room, reading by the fire. My middle daughter would immediately text back, "I miss No-Tech Tuesdays!" Once she even said, "I wish we did that more than one night a week."

Whodathunkit?

Were we legalistic about Tuesdays? Not at all. Some weeks our schedule messed it up and we'd switch it to another night or skip it altogether. But most weeks, Tuesday was the day.

No-Tech Tuesdays provided a true break from the bonds of technology. It helped us realize how much we all became enslaved to our phones, our TV shows, and other forms of entertainment media. Most of all, it allowed us to focus on face-to-face communication and the community people can experience when they hang out together, uninterrupted by the vibration in their pocket.

Consider trying it in your home.

Don't enforce it; suggest it. Google an article about today's kids attempting a media fast and share it with your kids. Ask, "Why do you think this is so difficult for young people today?" Once your kids attempt to assure you it's not hard, challenge them. Get the whole family to opt in.

You won't be disappointed.

Questions to ponder:

- Do you think your kids will be open to trying a "no-tech" afternoon and evening? How can you bring it up?

- Will it be difficult for you?

- When will you try it?

13 The Overnight Escape Strategy

On an eighteen-degree day in November when I was eight years old, my parents surprised my brother and me with an activity so simple and fun that it is still one of my fondest childhood memories.

School let out, and my brother and I routinely meandered to the car. It was a Friday afternoon, but we were young so we didn't have any plans.

Both my parents were sitting in the car, which was different than normal. My dad announced that he had gotten off work early, so he wanted to pick us up with Mom. We didn't think much of it. . .*until he passed the exit to our house.*

"Where are we going?" my brother asked.

"I don't know," my dad replied.

Our curiosity was sparked.

The next ten minutes became a guessing game.

"Church?"

"Grandma's?"

"The North Pole?"

Finally, they told us, "Nothing special. We're just going on a drive."

About an hour later they pulled up to a little hotel, which wasn't very fancy by any means, but for a family that never stayed in hotels, it was the Ritz! It had an indoor pool, which was heaven for my brother and me, living in Illinois at the time.

They opened the trunk of the car and pulled out some suitcases packed with everything we needed for twenty-four hours away from home.

For the rest of the afternoon, my brother and I were in swimsuits playing Marco Polo, seeing who could make the biggest cannonball splash, and finding out who could stay underwater the longest. Finally, after our skin was pruned, we made our way back to the hotel room, where we piled on the beds and watched TV together and ate takeout. . .right there on those ugly floral bedspreads.

It wasn't Disneyland, it wasn't New York City, but it was a blast!

My parents simply surprised us with a spur-of-the-moment getaway where we got a chance to hang out as a family.

Would this have worked when we were sixteen and seventeen? Probably not. We would have been bummed to be away from our friends. But for elementary school kids, it was perfect.

My wife and I practiced this occasionally with our own kids, taking them on various out-of-town excursions. My kids are a little spoiled when it comes to travel because I get to travel a lot with my speaking, so we've had to be extra creative, surprising them with a trip to Six Flags, or meeting up with another family in our church at a resort where our kids got to hang out with friends their age for a weekend.

These kinds of trips provided plenty of opportunities for them to enjoy their tech in the car and even in the hotel room. But they also provided plenty of time to engage in conversation as a family. In fact, sometimes we even involved tech in our bonding experiences. Each trip we told the kids to each create a playlist of ten songs that we would play on the drive. (My kids still love my youngest daughter's playlists the best. She has amazing taste!)

Figure out what this kind of overnight escape may look like for your family.

Questions to ponder:

- What kind of trips worked well with your family?

- What activities on this trip created a climate of conversation?

- How could you duplicate that climate now?

- What phone guidelines can you implement on this trip so your kids can enjoy their tech but not let it be a distraction? (See chapters on addressing the smartphone in the room and no tech at the table for ideas.)

- What would be a fun overnight escape with your kids?

- What kind of questions might you ask in the car? (See the bonus questions at the end of this book.)

14 A New Perspective of Back Talk

In a world where young people find it increasingly difficult to communicate face-to-face, today's parents need to help their kids learn to articulate their thoughts and feelings as often as possible—*even when it takes the form of back talking*.

Yes, you read that correctly.

Don't get hung up on the word *back talking*. Call it "respectfully speaking their mind," if you will. Perhaps it may sound like this in your home:

> "I thought I told you to clean your room."
> "You did tell me that, and here's why I didn't. . . ."

How many of you would be taking off your belt to teach this kid a thing or two?

At first glance, this kind of talk from your kids may seem disrespectful, or as some of us call it, "back talk." But what if I told you that allowing this kind of talk can not only open doors for healthy conversations, but it can help your kids learn to say no to drugs or alcohol.

Don't worry, I'm not advocating letting kids disrespect their parents. I'm advocating allowing kids to respectfully speak their minds. Not "type" their minds, but actually say what they are thinking through face-to-face communication.

Kids who can calmly and confidently disagree with their parents are actually 40 percent more likely to say no to drugs or alcohol than kids who didn't argue.

Sound crazy?

The University of Virginia conducted the study and published the findings in the journal *Child Development*. Dr. Joseph P. Allen studied 157 thirteen-year-olds, videotaping them describing their biggest disagreements with their parents. Some parents just laughed and rolled their eyes when they watched these videos. But the parents who wanted to talk with their kids about what they heard were the ones Allen described as "on the right track." The parents who allowed their kids to dialogue with them gave their kids practice handling disagreements.

Allen interviewed the teens again at ages fifteen and sixteen. "The teens who learned to be calm and confident and persuasive with their parents acted the same way when they were with their peers," he says. They were able to confidently disagree, saying no when offered alcohol or drugs. In fact, they were 40 percent more likely to say no than kids who didn't argue with their parents.

One of the biggest complaints I hear from teenagers is that their parents don't listen. Do you listen? Would your kids say you listen?

How can we expect our kids to put down their phones or tablet and engage in dialogue if we can't even provide a venue for said dialogue?

Consider the example of the parent telling her kid to clean his room. Is there a chance we may not know the entire situation?

Maybe we should listen to the rest of the story:

"I thought I told you to clean your room."
"You did tell me that, and here's why I was delayed. You also told me to feed the dog and finish studying for my SAT test. Molly looked hungry, so I fed her first. Then I went straight to studying because I figured that was the most important. When I finish studying in about fifteen minutes,

I'll get straight to cleaning my room. Is that okay?"

Gulp.

But let's be realistic. This probably doesn't happen too often. Some of us may experience much more flawed logic from our kids like this:

"I thought I told you to clean your room."

"You did tell me that, and here's why I didn't. I got a phone call from Taylor, and he really needed to talk. So I talked with him, and he wanted me to check out this comment that Chelsea posted about him. While I was checking that, I noticed that Jake posted lies about Katy, and so. . ."

Does this sound more like your kid?

This is the type of situation in which parents can rise up and respond back to their kids in a manner that corrects gently while still keeping the doors open for future discussion and avoiding angry outbursts.

Besides, when we give our kids the gift of *letting them be heard*, we can do one better than just getting them to clean their room. We can teach them to articulate themselves and stand up for what they believe.

Parents need to provide an atmosphere where our kids can freely express their thoughts and feelings. After all, that study revealed that "effective arguing acted as something of an inoculation against negative peer pressure."

That probably makes a lot of us think twice about simply responding, "Just shut up and clean your room!"

Questions to ponder:

- Name a recent time something like the above scenario took place in your house.

- What is your typical response in situations like that?

- How can you respond better next time?

- Do you believe allowing kids to speak their minds hinders teaching respect and obedience? How can you balance this?

15   The "Yes" Factor

Say yes to any opportunity to connect with your teen.

Any!

"Dad, have you eaten lunch yet?" my daughter asked me one day. She stood in the doorway to my office tapping the toe of her blue high-top Converse Chuck Taylor shoes.

Interpretation: "Will you take me to Rim's Deli and buy me that hot pastrami sub?"

My heart sank as I looked at the pile on my desk. I love my daughter, and I love Rim's Deli. . .but my plate was full. It was a quarter till noon, and even a quick glance at my inbox told me I was going to be working late that night.

I looked over at my daughter's stunning green eyes and sighed. "Absolutely," I said. "Let's go." I grabbed my jacket and pointed to her shoes as we walked out together. "Nice Chucks."

Sound irresponsible? It may have been. But I didn't care.

I recently tried an experiment. Whenever my teenage daughter initiated any connection, I never told her no. I made it my personal mandate to say yes every time. It didn't matter if I was in the middle of doing yard work or taxes, or even tackling a writing project due the next day. I slid it all aside and took the time to connect with my kid.

In all honesty, I probably improved this practice with the most urgency that year because the clock was ticking. My youngest was moving away to college that fall. I knew I was going to miss those moments.

I have reflected back on countless times when I was a young parent and my kids would ask me:

"Dad, do you wanna play video games?"

"Wanna play Barbies?"

"Wanna play a Barbie video game?"

So many times, I was too busy. (Can you hear "Cat's in the Cradle" playing in the background?) How I wish I could go back in time and change my responses.

I've never met a parent who reflected back on their own parenting and concluded, "I think I spent too much time with my kids." In fact, I've never met a parent who determined that they spent the perfect amount of time with their kids. The typical twenty-twenty look-back is "I wish I had spent more time with Michael," or "I could have paid more attention to Taylor."

So just say yes.

This becomes so much more important as your kids grow into adolescence. I'm not saying that younger kids don't need attention. They do. And we probably should say yes to them more often. But the fact is, most kids, as they grow into their teen years, seek connection with their parents less and less. Some of this is simply because teens get driver's licenses, jobs, girlfriends. . . . So in those shrinking moments when your teenagers actually ask you to connect with them, *don't miss out!*

Every face-to-face encounter you have with your kids not only helps you bond with them, it also reinforces the positive connection that can happen between two people when they look into each other's eyes and just talk. The more time our kids spend talking face-to-face, the better they'll be able to recognize facial cues, the more empathy they'll experience, and, as a result, the more socially competent they'll become. They may even be the only kid in their class who can maintain a conversation without pulling their phone out of their pocket. It all starts with you saying yes.

Questions to ponder:

- Can you think of a moment when you set aside your agenda to spontaneously connect with your child? How did that work out?

- Can you think of moments when you could have connected with your kids but were too busy?

- What would have happened if you would have just said yes?

- What would saying yes look like in your near future?

- Are there any adjustments you need to make to be there for these kinds of opportunities?

16 The Hot Tub Adjustment

When my brother and I were fourteen and fifteen, my dad made a purchase that revolutionized communication in our house.

He bought a hot tub.

Little did he know that this purchase would amend the communication climate in our home.

It's amusing how this purchase came about. Our neighbor was moving and asked if we wanted her hot tub. She couldn't take it to her new house, and the people buying her old house didn't want it. So she asked my dad, "You want a free hot tub? You can have the wood decking around it, too."

It took my dad two seconds to think about it.

"Yep!"

The next day, my dad, my brother, and I were at the neighbor's house carefully disassembling the wood decking. Eight hours later, we had the deck reassembled in our backyard. At that point, we became savvy as to why the new homeowners didn't want the old tub. Even though the decking was nice, this "free hot tub" was a piece of junk. It not only didn't work, but it was covered in mold and stains.

Next, my dad did something that I *never* saw either of my parents do. He made a spontaneous purchase. He went out that day and bought a new hot tub to fit into our newly installed decking. (Maybe he just didn't want a deck with a huge hole in it.)

A week later, our family was sitting in our brand-new hot tub looking up at the stars.

This became a regular practice before bedtime. My dad didn't want to go out and sit in the hot tub alone, so about thirty minutes before our bedtime, he would propose, "If you want to go to bed, you can. . .or you can stay up and go in the hot tub with me."

Yeah, the hot tub won over bedtime every night.

And that's when it happened.

We started opening up and communicating.

My dad looks back at that spontaneous purchase as one of the best he's ever made. To this day, he will tell us, "Before we bought the hot tub, deep conversations were sparse. But once we began our evening hot tub excursions, you guys couldn't stop talking. We'd get out under the stars, and you'd each bare your soul."

My dad still ponders the situation: "At the time, I probably thought the reason you talked so much was because I was such a good listener. But now that I reflect on the situation, I think it was just because you didn't want to go to bed."

My brother and my dad would agree with me—there was nothing magical about that hot tub. Sure, it was fun. And it definitely beat going to bed. But the reality of the situation was that the hot tub provided an arena where communication flowed easily.

And do you know what is magical about a hot tub today? Kids don't bring their electronic devices in it. (Yes, even the new waterproof devices don't fare too well in the heat.) When families get into hot tubs, there's nothing left to do but just sit and talk.

How often do you get to do that?

And who knows, when you are about to get out, your teenager might even grab his or her phone, take a quick selfie, and post it to Instagram with the caption "Hangin with the fam in the hot tub!!!" #liventhelife

Not too shabby.

As parents, we need to be on the lookout for these "communication arenas" where our kids aren't distracted by a vibration every ten seconds. A hot tub may just do the trick for you. And if a hot tub isn't in the budget, keep your eyes open for similar places where communication is cultivated.

Questions to ponder:

- What is your family's "hot tub"? In other words, what communication arena has worked with your kids?

- Where are some other places where technology doesn't interfere too much with communication?

- What kind of questions can you use to engage your kids in conversation in these arenas?

17 Froyo Exchanges

When my kids were young, conversation came easy. It's not hard to get a ten-year-old to talk with you. In fact, sometimes it's difficult to get one to shut up.

But most parents of teenagers would attest to the fact that as their teenagers became more independent, conversations grew a little less frequent. Sure, part of this may be the simple fact that teenagers often get driver's licenses, jobs, and girlfriends, all of which makes their availability for conversation sporadic. But many parents also experience a growing chasm conversationally.

"Hey baby, how was your day?"
"Fine."
"What did you have for lunch today?"
"Food."
"Any big plans tonight?"
"Nope. See ya later."

Sound familiar?

I wouldn't label my kids unsocial or rude, but I definitely noticed a difference in their communication as they hit adolescence. Conversations began requiring *effort*. The older they grew, the more I had to seek out settings where my kids would open up.

These venues varied with each of my kids. My son became a geyser of conversation if we just sat down and played video games together. (Two-player mode is an easy connection tool!) My oldest daughter loved shopping. But Ashley, my youngest—she was a hard nut to crack.

Then we discovered Big Spoon.

Big Spoon was the local frozen yogurt place on the way home from school. One day as we were driving by, my daughter looked out the window and said, "Oh, Big Spoon! That place has the best peanut butter parfait."

I didn't even know what peanut butter parfait was, but I almost caused an accident swerving into the driveway.

"Let's get us some froyo!"

A smile formed on Ashley's face. "Yes!"

Five minutes later, we were sitting across a table from each other stuffing our faces with peanut butter–flavored frozen yogurt, covered with peanut butter topping and sprinkles of mini peanut butter cups. It was diabetes in a cup!

But then something happened.

She began talking.

I never even had to ask a question. She just started talking about her day. The conversation flowed like the hot peanut butter topping.

Big Spoon was one of those places where Ashley put aside any drama, kept her phone in her pocket, and just talked. It became a "go-to" communication arena for us.

Did we go there every day?

No way. I'd have to run seventeen miles to burn off the calories in one of those cups. Besides, it wasn't cheap. The place allowed you to serve your own yogurt and pile on your own toppings. You pay by the ounce. Once I piled the crushed cookies and hot fudge on so high that my tasty masterpiece cost more than $12. (The cashier looked at me kinda funny that day.) But Big Spoon was a fun place to swerve into once every other week or so.

Is there something magical about frozen yogurt? Does peanut butter have endorphins that catalyze conversation?

Probably not. But for Ashley, Big Spoon provided a pleasant place where she could talk freely. Your local frozen yogurt place may provide the same. It depends on your kid. That's why this book is packed with countless different ideas just like this one. Chances are you'll discover many I don't even mention.

Where do your kids open up?

Questions to ponder:

- Name a time when one of your kids opened up and started talking with you. Was there anything about your location that cultivated that conversation?

- What other communication arenas might cultivate conversation like this for your kids?

- What are some of your kids' favorite places to eat? When is the last time you took one of your kids there for a one-on-one?

The Safe Source

If there's one thing that has hurt my relationship with my kids more than anything else over the years, it is my angry outbursts.

It doesn't matter how fun a dad I had been for weeks straight, whenever I let my temper get the best of me, my kids quickly withdrew, no doubt thinking, *I can't mess up—ever—or Dad will freak out.*

So far this book has been a blend of helpful practices (noticing, asking good questions), routines (coviewing, No-Tech Tuesdays), and stimulating settings (the hot tub, froyo splurges). Most of these have been things you can *do* to connect with your kids better. But this idea is better described as something you should *not do.*

If there's one thing that damages these connection efforts and destroys any of these efforts you have made, it's this: freaking out!

When Mom or Dad flip out, it communicates one thing: Mom or Dad is not a safe source.

Sometimes it happens when your teenager truly messes up. They violate your trust and disobey one of the guidelines you've set. If you're like most parents, when you discover this, the natural response is anger.

Anger isn't wrong; it's how we express our anger that often does the damage.

For example, if your kid sneaks his phone into his bedroom at night and stays up late chatting on social media, and you discover it the next day, the typical response is an explosion.

"If you think you are ever going to see your phone again, you're mistaken!" you may angrily shout. "I'm getting the sledgehammer!"

Yeah. Freaking out.

The problem with this is that now your kid knows you're going to overreact when they mess up, and that hinders the chance that they will ever come to you and open up about an embarrassing struggle or dilemma they're experiencing.

I'd better not ask Mom about this, they may think. *She'll just flip out!*

In my research for my book *More Than Just the Talk: Becoming Your Kid's Go-to Person about Sex*, I discovered countless reports revealing Google as the number one place young people go for answers about sex. Why? Because they know that Mom or Dad would freak out if they were to ask, "Mom, is oral sex wrong?"

So as a parent, you need to ask yourself where you want your kids going when they need counsel. You or YouTube?

Don't get me wrong. I'm not suggesting that you just let your kids do whatever they want. Far from it. I'm just proposing that you respond in love and understanding.

Let's say your kid violates one of the phone rules you've established. Instead of screaming and chucking the phone into the fireplace, try this:

1. **Buy time.** Give yourself time to think about how you want to respond. Delay the punishment. This has a double bonus. First, it gives you time to stop and think through a wise response. Second, the delay is a punishment in itself. Your kids won't want to have to wait for your verdict. They'll want to know right away. But don't give in. Instead, just tell them, "I'm sorry to hear that you messed up. I need to pray about this. So please just set your phone on the kitchen counter right

there while you go and do your homework. I'm going to think this over, and we can talk later."

2. ***Hear them out.*** After you've given yourself adequate time to think it over, sit down with your kid and ask him or her to tell you his or her side of the situation. Most teenagers feel like their parents don't listen and don't understand. Prove to your kid that you are willing to do both. You never know, you may gain some new information that will change how you respond.

3. ***Ask your kid's advice.*** Ask your son or daughter how you should respond to their transgression: "What can I do to help you learn from this situation?" This gives your kids a chance to come up with their own punishment. Who knows—maybe they'll choose something stricter than you even had in mind. Or maybe they'll come up with a better idea than you had. But most importantly, they'll feel like you are fair and just, maybe even approachable. The key is that they learn from the situation. Make that your goal.

Your kids will be much more likely to open up to you when they know you won't freak out. If you want to truly connect with your tech-addicted kids, then prove you're a safe source. Show them you care enough to listen and attempt to understand their world. Treat them with respect, and they'll be more likely to treat you with respect.

Isn't that how you'd like to be treated?

Questions to ponder:

- When was a time when you remained unusually calm when your child messed up or violated your trust?

- What did your child learn from you that day?

- Think of a time when you totally flipped out and overreacted. How did that work out for you?

- How could you have handled it differently?

- Which of the ideas listed above might be worth trying in your own home?

19) The Fire Pit Phenomenon

Remember the first time you roasted marshmallows around a fire?

Camping is one of those settings where people experience heaping portions of God's creation and minimal influence of technology.

My favorite camping locations are places with no cell service. This can be quite shocking for today's young people. If you've ever been to a location like this, it's amusing to see your teenagers walking around the woods holding their phones in the air looking for a signal.

But when the social media withdrawal symptoms subside and your kids realize they can't post the selfies they just took of themselves trying to pet a squirrel, they often will sit down and accept what nature offers at face value: beauty, serenity. . . stillness.

Then, when the sun sets, everyone begins thinking the same thing: *When are we going to light a fire?* Everyone loves the orange glow and welcoming warmth of a crackling campfire.

When my kids were just old enough to walk and talk, I would have them help me collect wood for the fire. I taught them how to kindle a fire and let it breathe. As they grew old enough, I let them build the fire, light it, and keep it stoked all night. This made them feel special and valued.

But the best thing about campfires is the social benefit. Campfires invite conversation. The warmth draws people around the fire, a natural sharing circle with everyone facing each other.

Add a few roasting sticks and marshmallows, and you've introduced food into the mix. Food always stimulates conversation. (Plus, it's really hard to hold your phone with sticky marshmallow fingers!)

One of my favorite campfire activities is telling scary stories. Young people love scary stories; just check your local movie listings and you'll see. It doesn't matter how many times my youngest daughter, Ashley, has heard the story about the guy with the hook for a hand who escaped the mental ward, she'll always beg, "Tell it again!"

Riddles like this one are another fun campfire activity:

"An almost empty room has an open window, curtains flapping in the wind. The table next to the window is empty. Water and broken glass are on the floor. Taylor and Morgan are lying dead on the ground. What happened? You have twenty yes-or-no questions to find the answer. Go!" (Answer: Taylor and Morgan are fish, and the wind blew their bowl off the table.)

Campfires aren't restricted to camping. Our family loves s'mores so much that my dad bought one of those portable fire pits for his backyard. Now, on an occasional clear evening, we'll all go down the street to his house to roast marshmallows under the stars. A little piece of camping in the 'burbs.

When's the last time your family sat around a campfire?

Questions to ponder:

- Have campfires stimulated conversation for your family?

- Where can you go and enjoy a campfire?

- Is there something in your own backyard that can emulate a campfire?

- What activities around a campfire might draw your kids into conversation?

20 The Playlist Connection

"Dad, do you like Hall & Oates?"

It was the last question I expected from a seventeen-year-old.

"Heck yes, I do!" came my answer.

That's how the conversation started. Next thing you know, we were scrolling through Spotify and listening to some of the greatest hits from the eighties.

My daughter Ashley loves music, so it has been a connection point for us over the years. It has manifested in numerous ways:

- *Home Sharing*—Back when iTunes was our primary library for music, we used its little feature called Home Sharing. When my kids were young, instead of giving them their own iTunes account, we "Home Shared." This was really fun because every time Ashley bought a new Tears for Fears song, I got it, too. In the same way, if I ever downloaded a new album, Ashley would text me something like, "*Lionel Richie's Greatest Hits*! Awesome!"

- *Name That Tune*—On road trips our family would often play Name That Tune. Ashley would usually DJ, playing the first few bars of random hits while the rest of us tried to guess the song and artist (one point for each). Ashley's taste and knowledge of music was so broad that she became quite the music aficionado. Every New Year's Eve, we hosted a big party with all of our friends, and Ashley would come up with a playlist for Name That Tune. Our friends would always look forward to that party. (They just couldn't wait for Ashley's 2016 playlist!)

- *Spotify*—When Spotify grew in popularity, Ash began posting some of her famous playlists. I joined Spotify for one reason only: to stay connected to Ashley's music.

It's funny how many hours Ashley and I have clocked together just playing music.

One night we were flipping through the channels and we landed on a Time Life infomercial for a CD collection called *The Power of Love*. It showed old music videos from Heart, Chicago, Air Supply, and others. Ashley and I never bought the CDs; instead, we just started making a Spotify playlist with every song that flashed across the screen. Ninety minutes later, we had an awesome playlist.

Playlists have served as a fun connection point for our family. Earlier in this book, I mentioned how our family would use road trips as a fun time for each of us to play a playlist in the car (one of my favorite playlists is still one titled "Ashley's AZ trip").

Playlists tell you a lot about a person. In my youth ministry days, I would give my adult volunteers a Y-jack so that they could plug two sets of earphones into any iPod or phone. On long bus trips or van rides, we would always sit next to kids and ask if we could "plug in" to what they were listening to. This provided amazing insight into their world. Sometimes we would even switch off, playing kids' playlists through the vehicle's radio. Kids would beg me, "Play my list!" These playlist connections always provided fun conversation about music and lyrics.

Some adults make the mistake of using situations like these as opportunities to lecture about inappropriate music.

This will stifle any chance of future dialogue on the subject. Kids will steer clear of the subject around these adults so they don't have to endure long lectures about "sinful" music.

If you come across inappropriate content, simply ask questions and let your kids come up with the answers. If the artist is singing about hooking up, simply ask, "Is he right?" Resist the urge to lecture. Always make discussions a dialogue, not a lengthy monologue.

If we can create a comfortable climate of conversation about any topic—music, social media, sex—then our kids will come to us again and again.

They may even ask a question like this: "Dad, what was your favorite song when you were my age?"

"Easy!" I'd answer. "Any song off Journey's album *Escape*."

Questions to ponder:

- What kind of music do your kids like?

- Do your kids feel free to play their music around you?

- How can you use music and playlists to springboard conversation with your kids?

21 The Serving Strategy

My church has a ministry called "Second Fridays," which helps feed people in our community who are struggling financially. Every second Friday of the month, volunteers show up early and begin preparing a meal for hundreds of hungry people.

This evening always provides great opportunities for the people of the church to connect with members of the community, many of whom are homeless. Dozens of volunteers from our church make this evening happen by cooking, serving food throughout the evening, and interacting with anyone who shows up.

Lori and I brought our kids several times to serve or clean up at Second Fridays, and the impact was remarkable. First, it opened our family's eyes to the community's needs. Second, it provided an opportunity to participate in a conversational ministry. In addition to meeting people's physical needs, we spent most of the evening simply talking with people and listening to their stories.

Today's parents should always maximize opportunities to keep the phones in the pockets and dialogue with people face-to-face. Service projects offer plenty of these moments. It's hard to dig a ditch, paint a house, or serve soup with an iPhone in your hand.

This isn't to say that people *can't* serve through technology. Sometimes churches and organizations give today's young people the opportunity to meet needs using their tech savvy—helping with sound, video, or social media, for example. As I said in the beginning of this book, I'm a huge advocate of using the tool in our pocket for good. We just need to teach our kids to be tech enabled, not tech dependent.

But even if your kids serve in the area of technology, look for occasional opportunities where they can put their phones in their pocket and get their hands dirty.

My mom volunteers at the local food bank in our town. She always talks about the teenagers who volunteer there— even if it is because their schools require a certain amount of community service for them to graduate. The experience is eye opening for many of these teens. Some sort food, bag groceries, and even help elderly people take food to their cars. It's an amazing opportunity for interaction that many of these teenagers would never experience in their own world.

It's great to look for opportunities like this that open up their eyes and expand their worldview.

A few years ago, my family bought blankets, water bottles, and McDonald's gift cards and gave them away to people we met on the street in downtown Sacramento. Experiences like these taught my kids to keep their eyes up and engage with people face-to-face.

Consider opportunities like these:

- Feeding people at a neighborhood homeless shelter
- Visiting the elderly in a nursing home
- Participating in neighborhood cleanup projects
- Tutoring
- Coaching
- Helping at the local food bank

The opportunities are endless. You can probably add countless examples to this list.

Serving changes lives, both ways. The person on the

receiving end obviously reaps benefit, but the person serving also gains amazing life experience, even more so when the project is kingdom minded.

When's the last time your kids have put their phones down, gotten their hands dirty, and served?

Questions to ponder:

- What opportunities have your kids had to serve? How did they respond?

- What service opportunities do you know of in your community?

- What can you do this week to help your kids take advantage of those opportunities to serve?

22 The New Kicks Occurrence

In my years as a youth worker, I used to go on campus once or twice a week to meet teenagers. This practice was grueling at times because teenagers are skeptical ("Who are you?"), painfully candid ("Why are you here? You're old!"), and undoubtedly narcissistic ("Oh yeah, well I. . .").

Nothing sharpened my interpersonal communication skills more than meeting kids on campus and trying to kindle conversation. Believe it or not, one of my most effective go-to discussion topics was *their shoes*.

Fashion is very important in today's youth culture, and shoes are a big part of that. No, this isn't something specific to girls. You can learn a lot about a guy from his shoes.

"Nice kicks"—a simple discussion starter I'd use.

"Thanks." And then, about 90 percent of the time, the teen or tween would tell me something about them. "I love my Vans. I wear them everywhere."

This usually gave me an open door. "Even to church?"

"Ha. Sure. If I went."

And the conversation began.

My daughters each value shoes greatly, and in completely different ways. Alyssa, my oldest daughter, loves heels and dress boots. Ashley, my youngest, loves Uggs and Birkenstocks (yeah, expensive taste).

These footwear choices are not only fun conversation pieces, but good connection points. If I ever want to get a guaranteed yes from my girls, it's simple:

"Do you want to grab a Jamba and then check out the sale at DSW?"

"Heck yes, I do!"

Yes, shoe shopping has become one of those safe settings, one of those communication arenas, where my girls keep their phone in their pocket and just talk with me face-to-face. As they look at shoes, I ask, "Where would you wear those?" The conversation can go anywhere at this point.

Will this work on every kid? Not at all. My son will tell you he loves his flip-flops, but then he'll change the subject. And he enjoys shoe shopping for about three minutes. If your kids are like this, then you may find yourself stopping by GameStop or Best Buy instead of the local shoe store.

The point is this: What do your kids value? They may be wearing it. Can you use that as a point of connection?

Questions to ponder:

- If your kids had $100 to spend, what store do you think they would go to?

- Do your kids open up and talk with you on these shopping extravaganzas?

- How can you use this to connect with your kids this week?

The Hunting Hush

Do you know what I like most about hunting?

The stillness.

If you've been hunting, you know what I'm talking about. People don't go duck hunting with their music blasting. You don't see anyone stalking a deer wearing their Beats by Dre headphones. And you certainly don't see hunters staring at their phones scrolling through their Insta pics.

Hunting requires you to be in tune with your surroundings. And that usually means "no tech."

My wife and kids will be the first to tell you, "Dad doesn't hunt." I'm not a hunter. I won't pretend to be. I don't own twenty guns and a big trophy room with deer heads mounted on the wall. But every time I've gone hunting with a friend or one of my cousins, I'm always intrigued by the hunter's appreciation for nature.

Sounds ironic, doesn't it: a guy who wants to kill an animal appreciating nature? But I've seen it again and again.

My dad does corporate training for volunteer organizations, including Ducks Unlimited and the National Turkey Association. He couldn't help but chuckle when he went to the first Ducks Unlimited convention. "It was full of hunters and environmentalists," he told me. "Two groups that you'd never fathom getting along with each other, unite to preserve the wetlands. One group, because they love the environment. The other, because they cherish a place where they can blow away ducks!"

If you've ever met duck hunters, you know that they often

study duck migration habits, practice duck calls, and spend immeasurable hours painting and perfecting decoys (arts and crafts for burly men). And when you get up at zero dark thirty to go hunting, the morning is divided into three stages: the hour-long hush as you crawl to the perfect ambush location, a mere seven seconds of shooting, and, finally, hours of laughing and conversation as you all collect your prizes and head home.

I've met a countless number of fathers who cite hunting as the best quality time they spend with their kids.

Note I didn't say "sons."

My friend Steve has two daughters, and Paige, his oldest, was his hunting buddy. In fact, I texted Paige with a hunting question when I was writing my book, *The Zombie Apocalypse Survival Guide for Teenagers*. She's my go-to hunting expert. (She's usually packing a knife.)

Fishing, hunting, camping—they all have similar characteristics: no cell service, beautiful surroundings, and a climate that cultivates conversation.

Do you take advantage of settings like this?

Questions to ponder:

- Describe a hunting experience you enjoyed. What kind of bonding took place?

- How would your kids respond if you suggested something like a hunting or fishing trip?

- When could you go?

24 What's Your Favorite. . . ?

Last year my daughter was sitting around with three of her friends, all of them huddled together and leaning over one of their phones and laughing.

My first thought was, *Wouldn't the fifty-five-inch TV be better for your necks?*

The laughing continued for what seemed like hours. I finally walked over and asked, "Okay. I give up. What are you laughing at?"

They began showing me ridiculous YouTube videos of goats screaming, and they were indeed hilarious. In fact, my wife came in about twenty minutes later and found me, huddled with my daughter and her friends, leaning over her phone and laughing my head off.

Sure, this isn't my favorite pastime. I'd rather lie back on my couch with my feet kicked up on my ottoman and watch something on the big screen.

But our kids wouldn't.

As a person who studies youth culture and trends, I closely watch reports about teens' entertainment saturation. Years ago, TV dominated their entertainment palate, with music and computer time filling much of the void. But now traditional TV viewing is shrinking. Some people misread these numbers and think that young people aren't watching their favorite shows anymore. Not true. They still love watching programming; they're just shifting to mobile viewing.

If you have teenagers, then I probably don't need to tell you this. How many times have you walked into a room to find your kid staring at their phone sideways and you ask, "What are you doing?"

"Watching Netflix."

In fact, some kids will watch a whole season of their favorite show in just a day or two (which is why Netflix "binging" can actually be a fun connection point—more on that later).

Kids love watching their entertainment on small screens. And even though I've seen some parents try to fight this, I suggest trying to use this as a point of connection. This is the same principle as the coviewing connection I shared earlier in this book, only on a smaller screen.

It's like this:

> "Whatcha watching?"
>
> "It's this guy who makes fun of stuff. He has a YouTube channel. It's pretty funny."
>
> "Show me your favorite one."

It's that simple.

In the early years of YouTube, my kids introduced me to Charlie the Unicorn, Julian Smith, Blimey Cow, and many more. Really funny stuff. Many of these moments provided little private jokes we'd quote around the house.

"Pass the *malk*."

Youth workers know this, and they use "mobile entertainment" as a connection point:

> "What's your favorite YouTube video?"
> "What's your favorite meme?"
> "What's your favorite Vine?"

Sometimes you can use these as discussion springboards:

"Do you think his rant was spot on?"

These discussions can reveal a lot to you about your kids' taste, and even their values.

Do you know what your kids are watching?

Questions to ponder:

- Can you name something your kids got excited about showing you?

- What are some of your kids' favorite things to watch on their phone?

- What is a question you could ask them that might initiate watching something together?

Pocket It

The number one complaint I hear from parents today: "My kid can't go five minutes without looking at her stupid phone!"

Not surprising. How can a sixteen-year-old with 387 Instagram followers possibly go an entire dinner without her phone buzzing at least once?

And what do teenagers do when they feel that buzz in their pocket? Like a rat drawn to a pellet, they habitually look at it. Right?

What do you do when your pocket buzzes?

Forget teens for a second. In a world where the average American adult spends eleven hours per day with digital media, you may want to think twice about your answer. Because researchers from Boston Medical Centre would argue that parents are setting the precedent with their own phone habits.

In their study, these researchers discovered:

- Seventy-three percent of parents used their phone at least once during a meal.

- One in three used their phones continuously during meals.

- The majority of children in these situations became restless and acted up to seek attention.

I gotta admit, when I read about this study, my first thought was, *I typically check my phone once when I am out at a meal.*

Gulp.

When my family is at home, we don't bring our phones to the dinner table. We've declared that part of our home a "no-phone zone," if you will (more on that later). Our family typically eats together and does dishes together. It's usually a fun time with lots of talking, laughing, and joking together. The phone doesn't interrupt this.

But many of us do let the phone interrupt our lives. It's like the phone connected to our walls twenty years ago. When that thing rang, what's the first thing we did? We got up and answered it. Forget that we were in a deep conversation with our family—"the phone is ringing!"

Urgent won out over important.

The same is true today. Our phone vibrates. . .and like Pavlov's dogs, we look. Why? Is your friend David's social media rant about the president really more important than your kids? I tell teenagers the same thing. Chances are, Brittany's Instagram post of her new American Eagle sweater isn't more important than your dinner conversation.

How about we just take our phones and set them aside? If you're out and about, pocket that thang! Why don't we all just agree to put our e-conversations aside for a few minutes and focus on the conversations we're having face-to-face first. And by "we all" I mean parents.

What would it take for you to ignore that buzz during dinner? What would it take for you to find some sacred times where you put the phone aside during the day and don't touch it, or better yet, don't even hear its buzz? (If you're retorting with, "I can't—my work needs to be able to reach me," then why not use the Do Not Disturb feature most smartphones have? Your phone will ignore all calls and texts except for certain numbers you determine in advance.)

Forget parenting for a second—think of what this would do for your marriage.

In her extensive research about how today's phones are becoming conversation killers, Massachusetts Institute of Technology professor Sherry Turkle discovered:

> Studies of conversation both in the laboratory and in natural settings show that when two people are talking, the mere presence of a phone on a table between them or in the periphery of their vision changes both what they talk about and the degree of connection they feel.
> —Sherry Turkle, "Stop Googling. Let's Talk," *New York Times*, September 26, 2015

It's probably time for us to remember what's important and put the phone aside for our family. Pocket it! Your example will speak far louder than your words.

Questions to ponder:

- Why do we always feel the need to answer a phone when it rings or buzzes?

- How often is a text, post, or phone call really more important than the conversation you're having face-to-face?

- Why do you think the mere presence of a phone on the table hinders the degree of connection between two people?

- What example are you setting when it comes to the use of your technology at home?

26 The Greasy Spoon Exchange

One day when I was seven years old, my dad offered to take me to breakfast before school. We talked, we laughed, we ate really good hash browns.

When breakfast was over, he said, "Let's do this every week."

And we did.

And when my own kids grew to the same age, I took each of them to breakfast, just as my father had taken me.

There's something about one-on-one time with your kids over food. This theme is woven throughout this book, packaged in various wrappers, but it's all the same concept. Parents need to discover venues where our kids feel safe, noticed, and comfortable enough to open up and just be themselves.

I've been working with teenagers for more than two decades, and I can tell you without hesitation that most teenagers don't have parents who seek out these kinds of arenas.

Where are these settings for your kids?

Have you considered being proactive about creating a weekly time for these kinds of encounters?

My town has a cozy little ma-and-pa diner that is known for its cheap breakfasts. My dad calls it a "greasy spoon." When I moved to the neighborhood a dozen years ago, they displayed a big sign that announced $1.99 BREAKFASTS. A few years later, it changed to $2.50; now it's $2.99.

Who can't afford two breakfasts at $2.99?

I brought each of my kids to this greasy spoon every other

week. I met with my son weekly, and I alternated with my daughters. This commitment took just two of my mornings each week—two mornings well spent.

When my kids eat, two things happen:

1. They don't check their phones for updates. Maybe this is a lucky by-product of our "no tech at the table" rule. But our kids know that meals are sacred.
2. Food catalyzes conversation. Maybe it's just us McKees. . .but we love food. It puts us in our happy place, and happy people are prone to get chatty.

If your kids like a certain restaurant, use this as a point of connection. (Good luck finding one with $2.99 breakfasts!) Make a weekly date. If your budget doesn't allow it, make it a coffee date. Your kids may actually prefer Starbucks to your town's greasy spoon diner. (More on coffeehouse couch connections later.) Just seek out a place where your kids smile and grow chatty.

Why not start this week?

Questions to ponder:

- What places do you know of where your kids like to eat out?

- What would keep you from scheduling a weekly time for this kind of engagement with your kids?

- When is a good time for you to do this?

- What is your first step to making this happen?

27 Fostering Controversy

"How was your day?"

"Fine."

"Are you excited about your soccer game?"

"Sure."

"I thought we'd make that homemade pizza you really like tonight. Cool?"

"Cool."

Does this line of conversation sound familiar? If it does, then you're probably a parent of a teenager.

Yes, this type of unengaged dialogue can be typical of adolescents. But it doesn't have to be. If you're getting one-word answers, consider one of these two thoughts:

1. Are you asking yes-or-no questions? Because if you are, then all day every day the answer will be one word.
2. Are you asking redundant, boring questions? In other words, do you ask your teenager, "How was school?" every day after school? Have you thought of changing it up?

If you really want to provoke your teenager to pocket their phone and engage in dialogue, then try using controversy.

No, I'm not telling you to bring up something raunchy or inappropriate. Just bring up something *debatable*. Maybe even something that was a tough decision for you as an adult. Bring it to the table and see what they come up with.

I did this when I worked with at-risk kids in youth ministry. We encountered sticky situations daily. So I brought one to my dinner table at home:

"We had a girl come to one of our leaders today and ask if she would give her a ride to get an abortion. She trusted this leader enough to come to her, and she was vulnerable enough to share this secret."

Then I asked my kids, "So what would you do?"

The discussion was priceless. How can we value this girl, value the relationship, *and* value the life of the unborn child?

After letting my kids wrestle with it awhile, I shared how my friend responded to this young girl. My friend had told her, "Yes, I'll take you, if we can make one stop to see my friend, and you promise to keep an open mind."

The young girl agreed, so my friend took her to get an ultrasound. When the girl saw the baby's beating heart, she changed her mind.

Life is full of sticky situations. Sometimes parents try to steer clear of these situations, thinking they are protecting their kids. Sadly, these kids don't get an opportunity to practice decision making under the love and guidance of our shadow. Why not engage in conversations like these while you still have some input?

- "Let's say a man gives his life to Jesus, but he is still living with his girlfriend. He wants to serve as a leader in the church. How should the church respond? What does the Bible say?"

- "You go to a slumber party with a bunch of school friends who don't go to church. When the parents go to bed, the kids turn on an HBO show that has a reputation for having explicit sex scenes. What do you do?"

Don't be scared to tackle controversial subjects when you see them.

Parents often ask me, "Are you saying we should bring this stuff up?" I always respond, "You don't have to bring it up. The world brings this stuff up all the time. All you need to do is be ready to engage in the conversation."

You can do this by using some of the questions I provided earlier in this book, like, "Is he right?"

Controversy provokes conversations, and it provides opportunities to teach our kids lasting values.

How can you argue with that?

Questions to ponder:

- Why do you think some parents are scared to talk with their kids about controversial subjects?

- What are some debatable subjects you've talked about as a family? How did that turn out?

- What controversial subject that you've seen in the news or in your community can you bring to your dinner table for discussion?

The Fan

"That is really cool. Show me how."

I'll never forget his words. My dad not only liked what I did, but he actually wanted me to show him how to do it.

Double bonus!

I had played the piano for seven years, but I really wanted to play the drums. When high school rolled around, I asked my parents if I could buy a drum set. Reflecting back on the experience, I can see my parents' hesitation. A drum set is a commitment to hours of noise daily. You might as well ask your parents if you can start a Harley Davidson repair shop in the garage.

But my parents shrewdly told me, "Jonathan, if you take classical piano lessons for one year, you can get a drum set."

I agreed.

Turned out, I thoroughly enjoyed both. Drumming was fun, but piano was mentally refreshing.

A funny thing happened. My dad became a big fan of my drumming.

My biggest fan!

I remember my first concert. My brother and I started a band with a few friends. He was on guitar, our friend Ken was on the keyboards, and I was on the drums (we had several singers throughout the years). My dad showed up to our first concert; I saw him standing there in the back. His mere presence was affirming.

During the concert, I did my first drum solo. It's funny to think about it as I look back. In my desperate attempt to be like the legendary John Bonham, my solo lasted almost five minutes, including a moment where I reached back to a bag of drumsticks and threw them one at a time, striking a lone cymbal on the other side of the stage.

When the concert was over, my dad had a huge smile on his face. "I loved those drums!" he gushed. "Wow! It was amazing. The crowd loved it!"

I'll never forget it.

"I loved those drums."

His words made an impact.

Sure, as a teenager I was probably more excited about the blond girl screaming in the front row than the middle-aged man standing in the back. But honestly, now I don't remember a single person at that concert—*except one*. And I'll always remember his words of encouragement.

In fact, later that week Dad asked me to show him how to play the drums. It was fun watching him try. It was an enjoyable bonding moment.

Can you remember the last time you offered your kid some simple words of encouragement? How about a time you asked your son or daughter to show you how to do something?

Today's young people love being deemed the expert at something. If you ever want to enjoy some fun one-on-one time with your kids, ask them to teach you how to do something they're good at. Do like I suggested in my earlier chapter about two-player mode: Walk in on them playing video games, take an interest in what they're doing, and simply ask, "Can I try?" Next thing you know, you'll be getting one-on-one training on how to kill bad guys!

Look for opportunities not only to take interest in their interests but to affirm them in those interests. Admire them. Catch them doing something well, and tell them you are impressed.

Become their biggest fan.

In a world where the overwhelming majority of people have a smartphone in their pocket, it's easy to offer some "online" encouragement: a nice comment about a posted pic or a kind text. But nothing trumps looking into your son's or daughter's eyes and affirming them to their face. Your face-to-face affirmation may be the only kind words they hear this week. And whom do you want your daughter hearing more affirmation from? You or that guy on the football team?

How can you affirm your kids this week?

Questions to ponder:

- Can you think of someone who affirmed you? What is the most affirming thing that person ever told you?

- What is something your kids do that you can affirm?

- What words can you say to affirm them?

No Tech at the Table

Many of the ideas in this book are ways we can embrace technology and actually use it as a tool for connection. That's okay. Technology is not a sin.

But *slavery* to technology is.

That's why it is beneficial to occasionally seek out settings where we simply put our tech aside and enjoy uninterrupted, 100 percent face-to-face interaction. In our house, one of these venues is the dinner table.

Our family adopted a policy years ago: *no tech at the table*.

It's that simple. Texts, Insta posts, tweets—they all can wait. Dinnertime is a precious time when our kids feel noticed and heard.

Apparently I'm not the only one lobbying for the importance of family dinners. Columbia University is in my corner. Year after year, the National Center on Addiction and Substance Abuse (CASA) has published studies about the importance of family meals.

Why would a group of scholars doing research on drugs and alcohol abuse write a report about families getting together around the dinner table? I'll let them explain:

> CASAColumbia has surveyed thousands of American teens and their parents to identify situations and circumstances that influence the risk of teen substance abuse. What we have learned is that parental engagement in children's lives is fundamental to keeping children away from tobacco, alcohol and other

drugs, and that parents have the greatest influence on whether their teens will choose not to use substances. Our surveys have consistently found a relationship between children having frequent dinners with their parents and a decreased risk of their smoking, drinking or using other drugs, and that parental engagement fostered around the dinner table is one of the most potent tools to help parents raise healthy, drug-free children. Simply put: frequent family dinners make a big difference.

The research is clear. The more often children have dinners with their parents, the less likely they are to smoke, drink or use drugs. Furthermore, the report asserts that kids from families who have infrequent family dinners (fewer than three per week) are

- twice as likely to use tobacco,
- nearly twice as likely to use alcohol, and
- one and a half times likelier to use marijuana.

CASA describes the family dinner as one of the most potent tools to help parents raise healthy, drug-free children. They conclude, "Simply put: frequent family dinners make a big difference."

A buzzing cell phone is a guaranteed distraction from the "parental engagement fostered around the dinner table" CASA described. Nip this interruption in the bud by simply declaring your dinners tech-free. That includes Mom and Dad.

Our kids will be enticed by venues that value their engagement.

Recently my kids were all home for Thanksgiving week. Alyssa's friend Mel came over on Tuesday night and joined us for dinner. We all laughed, stuffed our faces, and talked around the table. After Mel went home, Alyssa thanked us for inviting Mel. "Mel loves our family meals," Alyssa said. "She said they're special. They've made an impact on her. She told me she is going to make sure and have meals just like this when she starts her own family someday."

Lori and I were so touched. We don't think of our family dinners as unique. They're just cherished in our home. So tech can wait till after dinner. (And then after dinner, yes, everyone immediately checks their phone to see what they've missed!)

Questions to ponder:

- How would your kids' friends describe your family dinners?

- Do your family dinners foster conversation?

- How could you introduce no tech at the table in your home?

30   Kitchen Creations

Hands occupied with cooking and baking are typically too busy to pick up a smartphone.

That's what I noticed whenever my daughter Alyssa cooked.

When our kids became seniors in high school, we gave them each the opportunity to cook for us. This was more popular with some of our kids than others, and busy school schedules didn't always allow it. But one thing was for certain: Alyssa loved it. In fact, the closer she got to heading off to college, the more I would find her and Lori in the kitchen trying recipes together.

Now when everyone comes back from college for the holidays, I'm amazed at how excited my kids all get about cooking. Even my son. (Not long ago, he tried baking pumpkin cookies using real pumpkin—nothing out of a can.)

The nice thing about cooking is the dialogue that takes place as everyone works together. This doesn't necessarily mean technology is "banned" from the kitchen. Sometimes we even have an iPad open, trying a new recipe on Pinterest. But once ingredients are being chopped, diced, and added, the technology is usually put away.

I've already pointed out the importance of family dinners. But families can glean the same benefits preparing food.

Some dishes seem to create conversation better than others in our house. For example, there is an air of excitement in the McKee home when we have "Taco Night." Often you'll find several of us in the kitchen beforehand, adding our own genius to the ingredient list. Alyssa has a reputation for pouring her Cholula hot sauce on literally everything, and I add cheese to everything. (You can never have enough cheese!) This prep time is bursting with conversation. I think it's because McKees love tacos, so it makes them happy, and happy McKees are chatty McKees.

After dinner the same thing happens with cleanup. Dishes are never one person's job at our house—it's a group effort. One person clears, another puts away leftovers, two people work on dishes, and we all join on finishing up the last few pots and pans that didn't make it into the dishwasher.

I can't tell you why, but we have had more amazing conversations over dishes than almost any venue. *Any!* There's something about having just spent a meal together then working together to clean up. It's almost as if endorphins are released in McKee kids during cleanup, because they open up and talk more while doing the dishes than during any other venue I've listed in this entire book.

Cooking and baking aren't anything magical; they are each just another venue that brings people together. Technology is set aside and conversation always surfaces.

Try asking your kids to help in a small way next time you prepare a meal. If they enjoy it, ask them if they'd like to make the entire meal sometime. Give them the freedom to choose everything, and on your dime. Who knows? They could want to do it regularly.

And if you don't already do dishes together as a family, consider this practice in your home. Don't be discouraged if your kids aren't excited about talking when you first impose dish duty on the entire family. Give it some time. Conversation will come.

Questions to ponder:

- Does cooking create conversation in your house?

- Are some of your kids more interested in cooking or baking than others?

- What kitchen creations would draw people to your kitchen more than anything else?

31) The Wings and Rings Circle

Before someone accuses me of being too gender specific with my previous example of cooking and baking (and before I accuse that person of being misogynistic), allow me to give a more "sporty" example. (Call this "manly" if you will, but I'll stick with "sporty.") In my house, my girls are way bigger sports fans than my son. And one of the places I love to take them to watch sports is Buffalo Wild Wings, also known as "Bdubs" (derived from the acronym BWW).

Bdubs is a fun place for sports fans. For my family, it's also a great place for dialogue. Some of you might find it ironic that I am using an example of an establishment with more than fifty large TV screens mounted to the walls as a place to draw conversation out of a tech-obsessed kid. But that's exactly what Bdubs does with my daughters.

Bdubs isn't the only place where you can find this kind of setting. It's just a place where sports fans can get together over wings and onion rings and enjoy fun dialogue about something they love.

I recently taught a parent workshop at a church in Dallas and got a chance to spend the weekend with one of the pastors and his family. The family had a daughter and twin boys. The boys weren't more than ten years old, and they loved the Dallas Cowboys.

On that Sunday afternoon, I mentioned something about watching my Denver Broncos play, and they became fully engaged. These two ten-year-olds almost knew more about the Broncos than I did. When I went to the local sports bar with the family later that night, I learned why.

The establishment was a small, family-owned place with delicious wings. They had about ten TV sets, and the main one was tuned in to the Dallas game. The boys would ask their dad a question, and he would ask a question in return.

"Dad, why is Romo not playing?"

"You tell me. What happened last week?"

One of the boys piped up. "He got hurt."

"Yep," the dad replied. "So who is playing now?"

These two kids engaged in conversation about the game with their dad all night. I couldn't believe how much they knew about the game.

"There's a flag down, boys. What do you think the call will be?"

"Encroachment."

"Look at the replay. The defensive end moved!"

It was unbelievable.

For this family, sports was a connection point. And this local family sports bar was just an arena where the family enjoyed good food, NFL games on multiple screens, and plenty of conversation.

Many families have experienced these kinds of moments on occasion, but sometimes Mom or Dad isn't proactive enough to schedule them regularly. If you discover an arena where your kids naturally engage in dialogue with you, jump on the opportunity to do it again. Make it a Monday night tradition if you must.

Who serves the best hot wings in your city?

Questions to ponder:

- Are any of your kids drawn to sports? If not, what entertainment piques their interest?

- Where is a fun place you could go that might jump-start conversation with your kids?

- When is the next time you could take them to that place?

32 The *My Big Fat Greek Wedding* Method

Which do you think is a more effective way to teach today's young people how to make good decisions?

> "You should do this. . ."
> or. . .
> "What do you think you should do?"

It's funny how often parents, mentors, and youth pastors end up becoming the voice of "You should" or "You should not" in a young person's life.

> "Don't listen to that song; it's bad."
> "Don't drink alcohol; it's bad."

But what are these kids going to do when they get on their own—call us up from their college dorm and ask us what to do?

What if, instead of telling young people what to do, we began helping them learn to make decisions by asking them, "What *should* you do?"

Questions help us move from monologue to dialogue. Furthermore, they require our kids to come up with the conclusions themselves. After all, someday very soon they are going to have to do this on their own. Are you equipping them for that day?

My wife and I have found that this method of asking questions works much better with our kids. One of our kids in particular, is like Gus from the movie *My Big Fat Greek*

Wedding. The only way to get Gus to do something was to make him think of it himself. You may remember Toula pointing this out to her mom:

> **Toula Portokalos:** Ma, Dad is so stubborn. What he says goes. "Ah, the man is the head of the house!"

> **Maria Portokalos:** Let me tell you something, Toula. The man is the head, but the woman is the neck. And she can turn the head any way she wants.

You may remember the scene where they sat down with Gus and asked him for advice about who should work at the travel agency, while all along they knew the answer. They just needed Gus to come up with the answer for himself.

Many of our kids are just like Gus. We just need to lead them to discovering the answer.

We do this by presenting them with truth and asking questions. Yes, sometimes this will happen "on the fly." We'll be sitting at dinner or driving down the road with our kids and a teaching moment will arise. Our temptation in these moments is to lecture. Resist the temptation. Use fingertip questions, like the ones we learned in chapter 3 of this book, to get them talking:

1. What was the chorus of that song?
2. What does that mean?
3. Is he right?
4. How does this song mesh with your personal values?

Questions like this help us move from "You should" to "Should you?"

Parents, we can even use this when our kids approach us and ask us questions such as, "Dad, my teacher gave us a huge assignment, and now I can't go out with Brian. I promised him I wouldn't bail. What do I do?"

Don't always tell your kids what to do. Instead, lead them to the answer.

Ask, "What do you think you should do?"

Questions to ponder:

- Which do you use more, "You should. . ." or "Should you. . .?"

- How does asking your kids, "Should you?" help them?

- Why do you think they appreciate it more?

33 Netflix–Binge Bonding

Earlier in this book, I introduced the idea of coviewing to connect with your kids—not just movies or TV, but the content they enjoy on their mobile devices as well. One of the largest providers of said content today is Netflix. And Netflix "binging" is one of those activities young people undertake in heavy doses.

The question is, do we fight this or use it?

The difficult part of trying to use Netflix binging as a connection point is the nature of the activity:

- Today's young people usually do it alone, in their bedroom, their dorm room—anywhere they are just passing time.

- They typically do it staring at a small screen on their mobile device, which is not really conducive to coviewing.

- And coviewing by definition is more watching than talking, so it's not a tremendous conversational venue.

So is Netflix-binge bonding even worth it?

Absolutely.

Coviewing is so effective, in fact, that your kids' doctor has recommended it. The American Academy of Pediatrics consistently releases reports about the effects of entertainment media on young people. In many of these reports, they recommend that parents "coview TV, movies, and videos with children and teenagers, and use this as a way of discussing important family values."

Doctor's orders.

And just because coviewing involves a lot of sitting in silence, that doesn't mean it hinders bonding. Even hunting and fishing can necessitate extended periods of quiet without conversation. But activities like these provide a connection through the shared experience; plus, they are frequently followed by a time of conversation about the experience.

Coviewing can work the same way. Netflix shows are a fun source of entertainment to enjoy together. The shared experience is the big bonus. I call it *Netflix-binge bonding*.

Sometimes conversation will follow, but don't feel obligated to force the interaction. Remember, effective parenting includes both *bonding* and *boundaries*. It's okay to just *bond* with your kids and have fun. Everything doesn't have to be transformed into a life lesson.

So next time your daughter is sitting on her bed, staring at her screen (with spiderwebs forming around her), know that she may be watching Netflix.

Ask her, "Whatcha watching?"

That question is usually not a conversation starter. She'll probably just tell you the title of the show then keep staring at the screen.

"*Parks and Rec.*"

So ask one follow-up question: "Mind if I watch it with you?"

Her answer will either tell you a little about the show, or your relationship. If she's watching some garbage that she fears you'll disapprove of, then she may come up with an excuse not to watch it together. In the same way, if she really would rather just watch it alone, you may get the same answer.

Don't sweat it if this happens. Just try to keep the door open for next time. Ask, "Sometime?"

You'll probably get a "yes" to this question. (If not, you may have some work to do in the "bonding" category.) Embrace this. Try again a few days later.

When you get a chance to Netflix binge with your kid, don't force your rules on it—your show, your TV, your couch. Just crowd up next to your daughter right there on her bed and watch it the way she does. Get a feel of her world. Notice when she laughs or when she is emotionally stirred. Suppress the desire to lecture or correct, unless the show crosses blatant lines. Netflix binging is 90 percent bonding, 10 percent conversation starting.

Are you using Netflix for bonding?

What is your daughter watching right now?

Questions to ponder:

- Do you have a Netflix account? Amazon Prime? Hulu?

- What are some of your kids' favorite shows to watch?

- Have you tried coviewing any of these shows with them?

- How can you use these shows for bonding? Can you occasionally use them to springboard conversations about stuff that matters?

The School Shuttle Strategy

34

At my parent workshops, I often ask moms and dads, "What are some of the 'communication arenas' you discover where kids naturally open up?" It's so fun hearing the myriad of responses.

"Playing catch."

"Hiking."

"Playing Xbox."

Answers vary, but certain ones come up over and over again. And I don't think I've ever asked the question and *not* heard variations of one reply:

"On car rides to and from school."

"In our car pool, after we drop the other kids off."

"Our school commute."

It never fails. Parents everywhere seem to have luck with this particular setting. I know I have. Kids get in the car with Mom or Dad and just talk. Not every time, but frequently enough that parents see this as an effective communication arena.

This is just another one of those venues where two people are sitting side by side, not facing each other but trapped in conversation. In other words, there's nowhere else to turn. You're stuck with each other.

Well, today's generation has definitely discovered two common escapes from this setting: headphones and smartphones.

Many of us have experienced this. We pick up our kids, and they immediately turn to their devices instead of conversation.

So how do you prevent this?

Here are a few thoughts:

1. ***Establish a no-headphones policy when they're young.***
    This may sound harsh, but I solved this easily with my
    kids when they were six, eight, and ten. I came home
    with three gigantic "sound docks" for their phones—
    you know. . .those big speakers that their phones
    connect to so they can blast music. Sound crazy?
    Here's my logic: I'd rather hear what they're playing.
    When I brought the speakers home, I told my kids
    right then, "We're not going to be isolating ourselves
    with headphones in this house and in the car every
    day. At home you can use your sound docks to play
    your music. In the car, you plug into the car and play
    your playlists for everyone." We made the exception
    for long trips. On those kinds of journeys, headphones
    were allowed. I even bought them the headphones. But
    they knew that headphones weren't an option for the
    daily commute. Is this a little more difficult to begin
    at age sixteen? Sure. If your kids are used to wearing
    their headphones everywhere, it may take some time
    to get them used to being engaged in life without
    an ongoing sound track. The more you do many of
    these activities listed in this book, the more they'll
    enjoy positive experiences with no tech required. Give
    it time. Give them a reason to choose to take off the
    headphones and engage in the fun dialogue they can
    only experience bare eared.

2. ***If the smartphone comes out, ask engaging
    questions.*** I never made a "no smartphone" rule in the
    car. I tried to keep my rules to a minimum. So if my
    kids ever isolated themselves with their smartphone,

I'd just casually begin asking them engaging questions about subjects they enjoyed (see some examples in the Reviews & Qs section at the end of the book). I made it almost a game I played with myself. . . . *Can I get them to talk with me instead of their phone?* Usually I could get them engaged within a few questions.

The reason many parents struggle with this is they either don't care or don't try. If someone asked you the same boring questions every time you met ("How was your day?" "Any homework?"), you might ignore them, too.

Car rides provide you with a captive audience.

Are you bringing your A-game for this opportunity?

Questions to ponder:

- How is the conversation with your kids during car rides?

- During those commutes, how much effort do you put into the principles we've discussed so far in this book—noticing their world, asking engaging questions, and listening to your kids?

- What are some ways you can use car rides to engage your kids in conversation this week?

35 The Tandem Connection

In this book, I've already listed several outdoor activities that are very conducive for dialogue. One of the best of these activities is what I call the "tandem connection." This is simply because this activity isn't merely a setting where dialogue takes place; it's also a great team-building activity.

My friend Bob started a ministry a little over a decade ago called "Above and Beyond." Bob is an outdoor junkie. He loves rock climbing, cycling, skiing, and backpacking. Bob uses his love for outdoor activities to help people connect.

Bob's ministry was once donated ten tandem bicycles, and he began using them, particularly for father-son weekends. I went on one of these trips, and it was a fantastic experience—two people working together toward one goal.

That's the way tandem bikes work—both people need to pedal. One person can't sit back and relax while the other does all the work. The pedals move whether or not your legs want to. That connection links people together.

Cycling can be a fun experience in itself. Whether it's mountain biking or road riding, you'll notice something about people cycling together: they typically are engaged in conversation.

My hometown in Sacramento County has thirty-three miles of bike trail running along the American River. The trail is paved and has nice paths on both sides for walkers and runners. I've run along that trail for decades prepping for marathons and half marathons. That means I typically spend a minimum of an hour on the trail, usually more. In an hour, I probably encounter several hundred bikers whizzing by me. I always hear them coming.

Why?

Because they're talking.

The only silent bikers I encounter are lone bikers.

Tandem bikers are even more engaged with each other. The two riders have only inches between them, so conversation is easy. And that's what usually happens twenty minutes into the ride: *conversation*—often, deep conversation.

Once I went on one of Bob's tandem trips with a kid I was mentoring. The trip really helped the two of us bond. As we ventured out on long stretches of road together, the bike created a private setting where this young man felt safe to open up to me. We talked more on that trip than we had that entire year. Good times.

You may be thinking, *I don't have a tandem bike, and I don't know anyone with one.* Well, I don't know about your town, but mine has a bike shop that rents out tandem bikes. My wife, Lori, and I rented one once and had a great ride together. We laughed, talked. . .and then she screamed (we rode past a rattlesnake, and she freaked out!).

Tandems create conversations. . .and memories.

So that leaves you with only one question: Where can you get your hands on a tandem?

Questions to ponder:

- Have you ever been on a tandem bike or kayak? What did you find enjoyable about it?

- What outdoor activities do your kids enjoy?

- Why do you think tandem bikes provide such a good arena of conversation?

36 Resisting the Stalker

One of the most common questions I hear from parents at my workshops is "What software do you use to track your teenagers' phones?"

I think I disappoint many of these parents when I tell them, "I don't."

Let's look at this big picture for a moment. We have two types of parents. There are the overpermissive parents who buy their kids a smartphone at age eight and never set a single boundary. On the other extreme, we have the overprotective parents who don't let their kid go anywhere or own any technology, hoping they'll be safe from the evil clutches of the world.

Here's the problem: neither extreme works. And following your teenager's every move is tiptoeing toward the overprotective extreme.

Don't get me wrong. I'm not suggesting you let your kids do whatever they want. In fact, I'm a huge advocate for helpful boundaries, especially for younger kids. But as they grow older, we need to teach them discernment, and they'll never learn to discern if we make every decision for them. That means parents need to slowly release their grip as their kids get older.

That means *no stalking!*

Accountability is a good thing. Stalking is a bad thing.

One of the ways you can hold your kids accountable is by requiring them to provide you with all their passwords when they are young and they first get their phone. No tracking software, no spying on them, just passwords. That means Mom or Dad can look at their young teen's phone whenever they want. My daughters didn't like this, and they were rather vocal about it. But whenever we discussed it, I always stumped them with this question: "When is the last time I looked at your phone?"

The fact was, my girls were trustworthy and I didn't need to check their phones. But I had the ability to do so at any time. They learned that the more they demonstrated trust, the more freedom they enjoyed.

Parents also need to be careful not to smother their kids in the social media world. We all know parents who seem to live on social media and comment on literally every post, especially their kids' posts. It's parents like these who provoke kids to leave Facebook and seek out new social media platforms, ones Mom and Dad aren't watching.

The scary thing about this is that some of the more "private" social media platforms are dangerous. Young people are fleeing accountability and landing in "anonymous" social media playgrounds where they feel as if they can post anything with no consequences. Many young people learn hard lessons, like the reality that nothing we post is ever truly anonymous, and many of said posts come back to haunt them.

If Mom and Dad chilled in the first place and stopped smothering their kids online, then kids wouldn't feel as compelled to flee.

One of my blog readers, a youth pastor, told me stories about some of the parents of kids in his youth group. One mom constantly posted embarrassing photos of her kids. She thought it was fun, but her daughter was in tears over some of the pics. Another mom posted something about her son snuggling in bed with her that morning—a harmless incident, until it was posted publicly and led to him being ridiculed at school that day.

In a culture where almost half of teens have been harassed online, parents need to use wisdom and think twice about their posts. And if they want their kids to experience the freedom to earn trust, then Mom and Dad may want to back off on the stalking as well.

What does walking this line look like?

- Be involved in your kids' lives enough that you get to know their world through conversations, not spying.

- Require passwords from your kids when they're young. Start strict, then give them an increasing amount of freedom as they mature. Passwords provide accountability without a "big brother is watching" feel.

- Feel free to engage in social media with them—get an Instagram account and *occasionally* "like" their photos. Resist the urge to comment on every photo. Give them enough slack so they forget you're one of their followers.

- Engage in frequent conversations about social media values—*dialogue*, not *monologue*. Ask questions and then do more listening than talking.

- Stay current by reading about youth culture and technology (my blog and Youth Culture Window articles on TheSource4Parents.com are both great resources to keep you informed).

Guardrails can help your kids stay on course. Shackles, however, only bind your kids from ever learning to make decisions on their own.

For more on what realistic guardrails look like, take a peek at my book *Should I Just Smash My Kid's Phone?*, available on TheSource4Parents.com.

Questions to ponder:

- I described two extreme parenting styles above: the overpermissive parent and the overprotective parent. Which extreme do you gravitate toward? How's that working for you?

- Where do you think the perfect balance lies?

- Where is the line between spying and accountability?

- What are some rules or boundaries you might want to implement or change in your house?

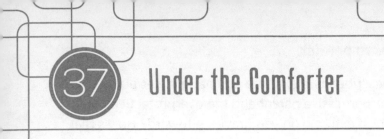

Under the Comforter

"Daddy, did anyone ever pick on you at school when you were my age?"

Questions like this always seemed to come from my daughter Ashley at bedtime as she stared up at me from under her warm comforter. Sure, she probably was just desperate to stay up, but I didn't mind. We had some amazing conversations just before bedtime.

This may sound like a no-brainer: *Yes, Jonathan. Simple. Talk with my kids as I put them to bed.* But let's be honest. It doesn't always happen. Especially as they get older.

Here's what this situation typically looked like in my home:

As my kids grew to high school age, bedtime was less official. A kid would get home from sports, eat dinner, and then disappear upstairs for long hours of homework. Sometimes Lori and I would finally be relaxed down on the couch together and we'd hear a voice from upstairs yell, "Goodnight, Dad and Mom. I'm going to bed now!" And then we'd hear a door shut.

Put yourself in my position for a moment.

- You've had a crazy busy day.
- You're sitting down for what feels like the first time all day—with your feet up.
- You're in the middle of an episode of your favorite TV show.
- You're engaging in quality, uninterrupted bonding time with your spouse.

- Your kid is old enough to put herself to bed; plus, she sounds like she just wants to go to bed without you interrupting—right?
- It's easy to convince yourself to just let your kids go to bed by themselves.

Here's my advice: Get your lazy butt up and go kiss them *good night!*

This doesn't mean you have to force a conversation out of them. It truly may just be a quick kiss, a prayer, and "Good night, baby. I love you!" But it's worth it. Show up at their bedside each night. They may not even show you appreciation then, but it's what they need. They need to know you're there for them.

You'll put them to bed a dozen times, and they won't say but two words—usually just "Good night." But then, on that thirteenth time you put them to bed, they just may look up at you from underneath their blankets and ask, "Mom? Did you ever like a boy and he didn't like you back?"

That's the crazy thing about *quality* time. It requires *quantity* time. You've gotta show up over and over again to be there for those occasional quality time moments.

If your time is limited, then the bedtime setting is a good investment because it's often potent with conversation. It's one of those arenas where communication is commonly cultivated. The bed is a safe place where kids can bury themselves under cozy covers and escape the pressures of the cruel world around them. My girls often asked some pretty deep questions when they were burrowed in the comfort of their sheets and blankets.

Where do *your* kids feel safe?

The bed is also a place where technology is put away for the evening (or should be—see my chapter about the family docking station), so parents don't have to worry about the interruption of technology.

Comfy surroundings, no tech, a caring parent at their side—what more could a kid ask for? It's the perfect storm for meaningful conversation.

Are you making use of this opportunity?

Questions to ponder:

- Why do you think young people often open up at bedtime?

- Do your kids? Why or why not?

- What can you do to create a safe environment where conversation is easy?

38 Water Like Glass

Camping, hiking, cycling, kayaking—there's something about being outdoors that helps kids lift their eyes from their phones and absorb the beauty of their surroundings. One of the best places to enjoy this kind of majestic isolation is from a boat gliding across smooth water. It doesn't matter what kind of boat: kayak, ski boat, fishing boat. The vessel isn't the focus.

The surroundings are awe inspiring. Have you ever seen a goose take off in flight from a lake, dipping the tips of its wings in the water as it attempts to gain altitude? Have you seen tiny baby ducklings paddling one after another, trailing behind their mother? Have you seen water so smooth that the reflection of the surrounding hills makes you question where the land and water meet?

If you ever have an opportunity to take a boat out on quiet waters, don't miss out on the experience. I've heard many a parent testify how their best family bonding time was on a ski boat, houseboat, or canoe trip.

My friend Scott tried to talk me into kayaking with him for years, and I finally gave in. In hot Sacramento summers, the temperature of the air hovering just above Lake Natoma is about five to ten degrees cooler, and the view is breathtaking. As I paddled across the water, feeling the cool breeze on my face, my first thought was, *I have to take my family out here.*

Lori and I rented kayaks several times and enjoyed them so much that we eventually bought two. This opened the door to new recreational possibilities for the McKee family. During the spring and summer, you'll see our tandem kayak on the roof of our Pathfinder almost daily. My daughters both occasionally paddle with me. Alyssa, my oldest, even entered a race with me in which we both ran, cycled, and kayaked (they call it the no-swim triathlon). Over a period of months, we trained regularly together in the tandem kayak, the two of us working together to paddle in sync. Every one of those times was laden with conversation.

My friend Matt grew up waterskiing with his family as a kid. When he started his own family, they bought a ski boat. Matt takes the boat with them on camping trips throughout the year. They've invited our family to join them on several occasions.

And the great thing is, the teenagers never pull out their smartphones during these trips.

Last summer I took my teenagers white-water rafting (so the water wasn't exactly as smooth as glass). My kids were teens, so I sweetened the deal by telling them they could each invite a friend. The day was amazing. No phones at all, just rafting down Class III rapids with a guide, working together as a group. Great memories! Afterward we all went out for burgers, laughing and talking about the day.

Outdoor recreation has a funny way of capturing young people's attention, probably because they are social creatures at heart. They are glued to their devices largely because they are attracted to the connection said device provides to friends old and new.

We weren't that different when we were their age. Think about it. How many times did your mom or dad have to say "Get off the phone!" The difference was, ours was connected to the wall. (And it wasn't also a computer, a TV, a music player, a game system, and a camera)

So look for outdoor activities that naturally engage your kids in conversation. Water activities are some of my personal favorites. These activities can be so engaging, you may even be able to go an entire day without having to say, "Get off your phone!"

Questions to ponder:

- What outdoor activities does your family enjoy?

- Why is it that so many young people love water activities?

- What would you have to do to bring your family out on a boat in a serene location?

The Coffeehouse Couch Connection

It's unprecedented. There's nothing like it. Young people's love for coffee and coffee shops is something unique to this generation.

Think about it. Where did young people go in the 1980s to study, to meet others. . .to simply hang out? McDonald's? The video arcade? Detention? (It worked in *The Breakfast Club*.)

Today? Not even close.

Nothing parallels young people's love for the corner Starbucks in America. Check it out for yourself. Visit your local Starbucks, Tim Hortons, or ma-and-pa coffee shop in your town and look around. Better yet, ask your daughter (girls enjoy this more than boys), "Wanna go grab a Starbucks?"

Starbucks is really good about providing a cozy atmosphere conducive for conversation. High-top tables, couches, tables for groups of all sizes. The setting is perfect for conversation.

That's the unique element about coffee shops. The climate carries an assumption that dialogue will take place. Sure, you'll find some people there reading or studying by themselves. But when two or more are gathered. . .*they're talking*.

My daughters got the Starbucks itch a few years ago. In fact, they even downloaded the Starbucks app on their phones (brilliant move by the company). After a certain amount of purchases, their status elevated to the point where now they can get free coffees and other benefits. So whenever I offered to take them to Starbucks, I sweetened the deal: "I'll add money to your app, and we'll pay for it that way." I paid the exact same amount of money I was going to pay, but they got the credit. This always made them more eager to go with me. And every time we went. . .*conversation*.

Let me help you understand something: I don't drink coffee. I can't stand it. But I like sitting on a plush couch with my daughter laughing and sipping lemonade. I'd be a fool not to use the coffeehouse couch connection with this generation. When I go, I just order water or eat some of their delicious baked items (not good for my waistline, I admit). Most coffeehouses have hot cocoa as well.

When I'm in Canada, I do the exact same with Tim Hortons. Canadians always ask me, "Do you want to go get a Timmy's?"

And I always answer, "Youbetcha!"

As a youth worker, I use the coffeehouse couch connection to connect with other teens as well. When in doubt, I suggest Starbucks. I can count on one hand the times a kid suggested something else.

Coffeehouses can be easier on the budget than breakfasts or dinners. Two coffees only cost a few dollars. Very affordable.

How much is a conversation with your kids worth?

Questions to ponder:

- What coffeehouses seem to be popular in your town?

- Have your kids ever shown interest in going there?

- What do you think your kids would order if you brought them there?

Memory Lane

When I was a kid, my dad recorded everything on a Super 8 camera with no sound. Film was expensive, and setting up the projector was a pain. That's probably why the films of my childhood jump from me at five years old to seven years old to ten years old. . . .

Contrast that with when my kids were born. We had a video camera ready from birth (with strict instructions from my wife not to film the actual birth). If you go through those old tapes, I have a two-hour tape of the first few days after my son was born, another tape of the next six weeks, another of his first year.

Nowadays, we don't even need a video camera. We just use our phones and edit our recordings on our tablets or laptops. The more technically savvy we become, the more we have record of our kids' childhoods.

And guess what? This generation likes to see themselves.

Something happens whenever I pull out the old movies of when my kids were young. The kids sit down and watch them with us.

Yes, I'm a little strategic with how I do it. I don't pounce on them when they walk through the door from school and ask, "Wanna watch family movies tonight?"

In fact, I don't ask them at all. I just pull out the old videos as the last dish is being washed, press PLAY, sit down on the couch, and don't say a word. Four out of five times the kids will sit down with me and begin asking questions:

"How old was I in this one?"

"How long did we live in that house?"

"When did Alpine have her puppies?"

"Why did you wear those hideous shorts? Did you actually go out in public like that?"

Whenever I start a walk down memory lane (and I don't do it but a few times a year), the kids almost always are drawn in.

Now that my kids are all out of the house (Ashley left for her college freshman year literally as I was writing this book), they seem even more eager to walk down memory lane with us when they come home to visit. Ashley will go to the drawer on her own and pull out the family movies and start watching them.

"Dad, wanna watch these with me?"

One thing I like about these moments is that conversation comes easy. Lori and I don't have to ask too many questions. In fact, the kids ask most of the questions. Typically, we just hit PLAY, and the questions start rolling.

And yes, I did go out in public wearing those shorts. They were cool! Everyone was wearing them at the time.

Questions to ponder:

- What good family memories do you have on video?

- Do you have family movies saved in a format that allows you to play them easily?

- How can you be strategic about playing family movies so that your kids might sit down and watch them with you?

Here Are the Keys

My cousins grew up on a nine-hundred-acre ranch. Cows, horses, chickens. . .and plenty of wide-open spaces. That's probably why Dusty got to drive on the property when he was about twelve years old.

It's funny seeing a twelve-year-old behind the wheel of a full-sized Chevy truck. But you should have seen that kid light up when his dad tossed him the keys and said, "Wanna drive?"

Kids love taking on adult responsibilities. Think about when your kids were young and they first got out of diapers.

"I get to wear big-boy pants!"

Kids assert their desire for incremental independence with even the smallest tasks:

"I'll pour my own milk."

"I want to light the candles."

"I can carry it by myself."

This prospect frightens many parents because we immediately think of the dangers. We've all had to clean up spilled milk. But stop and think about this for a second. What's worse, a little spilled milk or a kid going off to college who has never learned how to make his own bed?

Don't get me wrong. I'm not suggesting you break the law and let your twelve-year-old drive—*in downtown Chicago*! I'm proposing that you eagerly embrace opportunities to let your kids engage in activities that demand adult responsibility in the safety of your shadow.

Kids get an opportunity to feel like a grown-up when they do simple activities like these:

- Driving the boat
- Operating the saw
- Pushing the shopping cart
- Using the stove or the oven
- Pushing/driving the lawn mower
- Turning the TV/entertainment system on

The fun aspect of every one of these activities is that they monopolize your kids' entire attention and require them to put those mobile devices away.

Let me say that again in case you missed it. These tasks will make your kids leave their phones in their pockets.

Sign me up!

Obviously these tasks are going to vary by age. Your sixteen-year-old is just going to stare at you as if you're an idiot if you ask him, "Do you wanna push the shopping cart?"

But try tossing him the keys to the family SUV when you're about to drive somewhere with him. My guess is you'll get a completely different reaction. (And you're guaranteed an entire car ride in which he can't look at his phone—it's the law!)

Chances are, this experience will be a fun bonding moment for the both of you. Who knows, maybe he will even engage in a little conversation to pass the time.

Questions to ponder:

- What "grown-up" responsibilities or opportunities have you given your kids?

- How did they respond?

- What are some opportunities you think your kids would really respond to?

Peak Exchanges

I've already highlighted several outdoor activities in this book. Most of them have these common denominators:

- Beautiful scenery that tends to give kids something to look at other than their mobile devices
- Remote locations without a Wi-Fi signal
- Unique settings that provoke conversation naturally

One of my favorite ways to achieve all those elements and more is a one-day hiking trip.

I know, some of you may live in a city where you're not exactly close to a nice mountain trail. But let me quickly interject: I travel all over the world and usually hit more than twenty U.S. cities each year. One of the first things I do in most locations is scout out some running trails. Even the most urban areas (Chicago, New York, Baltimore) have some amazing trails or riverside pathways that are perfect for these types of ventures.

In my hometown in the suburbs of Sacramento, we live less than a hundred miles from Lake Tahoe, which is nestled in the middle of the Sierra Nevada. This means we are about a ninety-minute drive from some amazing hiking trails with one-thousand-foot gains and amazing views.

Ever since the kids were young, we have taken them with us on small hikes. Kids love these kinds of adventures. They each wanted to find the perfect hiking stick and take turns walking the family dog. These hikes were ripe with conversation.

As they grew into their teens, naturally they weren't jumping for joy when we suggested a family hike. So, often we would strategically sweeten the deal and word it like this: "This Saturday we're thinking of heading up near Truckee to climb to Loch Levin Lake and swim around. We'll stop for pizza on the way home. Would each of you like to bring a friend?"

It wasn't really a "You are required to go," but it wasn't really a "Do you want to go?" either. Frankly, they typically just began thinking about which friend they wanted to bring with them.

The hikes were amazing. We'd hike three to five miles, arrive at a desolate lake, swim, dive off rocks, explore new trails—it was always an adventure. Many of the kids' friends had never been on such an escapade. Their excitement always made my kids even more enthused about these kinds of ventures.

And guess what happened during the hours of hiking and swimming and exploring in a location void of any cellular signal?

Talking. . .

More talking. . .

Even more talking. . .

Sometimes when we'd arrive at the peak of a mountain we'd just scaled, we'd all just sit down and take in the 360-degree view. Something about these moments always provoked some amazing conversations. Peak exchanges, I called them.

Then we'd all pull out our phones and snap pictures in eager anticipation of posting them once we got down the hill and got a cell signal again.

Questions to ponder:

- Is there a place near you where you can take your kids on these kinds of walks or hikes?

- Why do you think starting these activities when kids are young helps?

- If you have teenagers, how could you "sweeten the pot" so that they might want to take one of these ventures?

43 The Mani–Pedi

Lori and I had the privilege of going to Hawaii for our twenty-year anniversary (and of using some saved-up hotel points to stay at a nice resort). On the second day, my wife asked me, "Wanna get a pedicure?"

I raised my eyebrows. "Me? But I'm a man!"

She laughed. "You won't get your nails painted. A pedicure is so much more than getting your nails done. It's like a long foot rub with a—"

I interrupted her immediately when I heard the words "long foot rub."

"I'm in!"

She laughed again. "I knew you'd want one!"

Lori and I sat in reclining chairs with our legs up for about thirty minutes while two ladies scrubbed our feet, rubbed them, massaged them—*it was wonderful*!

Now I get a couple a year.

And now I also know what my daughters have been enjoying all along.

About five years ago, a new nail salon moved into the strip mall by our house, advertising: $39 Mani-Pedi! Lori told my girls, "Let's try it." The three of them made an appointment and went together. About ninety minutes later, they came back with big smiles on their faces—and freshly painted nails all around.

Three people at $39 each—this wasn't something they could do all the time. But that didn't stop the three of them from doing their own at home. In fact, my girls bought their own little portable foot-washing station with cleaning supplies and a unit that blew tiny bubbles around your feet like a miniature spa. On certain evenings, the three of them would disappear into our master bath for what seemed like hours (probably about the same time it took me to watch *Rambo* or *Terminator* in the other room, trying to boost up the testosterone content in the house) wash each other's feet, and paint each other's nails.

Whenever I walked in on their little homegrown mani-pedi sessions, I saw the same thing I witnessed in the salons: *conversation*. There's something about having their feet up and being pampered that makes people relax and open up. Plus, when they were doing each other's nails, their hands were too busy to pick up their mobile devices. Nail painting monopolized their attention.

Always be on the lookout for activities that require the use of hands. These are perfect for occupying and connecting with the smartphone generation.

Ever since I accepted the mani-pedi into my heart, I have enjoyed this experience with them. It's something we've done in conjunction with vacations multiple times now. If we're going to be spending a week on the beach somewhere, someone in our house will suggest, "Mani-pedi!"

I'd be the first one to say, "Yep! I'll make the reservation"—which they don't mind, because they know I'll pay.

The key is to make an appointment so you can make sure you get two chairs next to each other. Some places can only do one person at a time, but we don't use those places, because we want the social aspect. It's no fun getting a mani-pedi alone.

It's also key to get both the manicure and the pedicure, because guess what happens if your kids just get a pedicure? Then their hands are free! And what do you think your teenagers will pull out of their pockets when their hands are free?

So Mom. . .and maybe even Dad. . .consider the mani-pedi as a tool for connection. (Plus, who doesn't want a free foot rub!)

Questions to ponder:

- Who in your house might be most likely to enjoy a mani-pedi?

- What other activities can you can think of that require hands and therefore minimize the chance of your kids pulling their phones out of their pockets?

- When is a time you could initiate one of these activities and use it as a setting for conversation?

The Cookie Dough Connection

In the McKee house, cookie dough is like a tractor beam. It draws people out from every corner of the house.

Earlier in this book, I shared how cooking and baking can occupy hands, creating an arena where conversation takes place. For my family, making cookie dough provides one of those settings.

The reasoning is simple:

- We eat the dough with our hands—which prevents the kids from having their phones out.

- We all love cookie dough, so that puts everyone in a good mood. Again, happy McKees are chatty McKees.

- Cookie dough often gets us all in a playful mood. Play is an important part of bonding.

Don't underestimate the power of play and laughter. Having been in youth ministry for twenty-five years, I've used "play" to open up doors with the toughest of kids. Years ago I worked with at-risk kids in very tough neighborhoods, and I used play and laughter to break down many walls.

It's Bonding 101: when families laugh and play with each other, they grow closer.

Cookie dough always instigates a fun battle in our house: Lori versus the four of us. Lori makes the dough, and the rest of us try to sneak handfuls of it before she bakes it all. This typically provokes a little chase around the kitchen.

Lori strongly believes that cookie dough is worse for you than baked cookies. She has a variety of (weak) arguments: the salmonella dispute, the "raw dough has more calories than cooked dough" argument, and then the plain ol' line of reasoning, "Why are we even making cookies if you're going to just eat all the dough?"

In twenty-five years of marriage, Lori has lost every one of these battles—probably because she's typically outnumbered four to one. Sometimes she just brings us all a big spoonful of dough, not because she is giving in, but because then at least she is controlling the quantity of our intake.

But cookie dough seems to have magical powers in my house (other than the power to make us all feel guilty for our fat intake!): the power to gather everyone in the same room.

Always be on the lookout for anything with this kind of draw for your family (I hope this book has given you a few ideas).

The conversation that springs from these gatherings is often related to the activity taking place. For example: often when our family is eating cookie dough, someone will chime in with this question: "What are your top five desserts, in order?"

This is fun to hear, and it gives us good ammunition if we ever want to surprise the kids with a special dessert for their birthday or other celebration.

What draws your family to the kitchen for these kinds of fun conversations?

Questions to ponder:

- What kind of food or dessert might draw your family together?
- What kind of setting puts your family in a playful mood?
- Why do you think laughing and playing creates a bonding moment?
- How can you try to create some of these moments this week?

Poolside Moments

"What is your favorite TV show?"

It's a question I ask a lot of people today when I'm just shooting the breeze. In a country where families spend upward of five hours a day with the TV on, it's usually an interesting item of discussion. That's why I'll never forget my friend Eric's answer:

"We don't watch much TV. We just hang out in the backyard around the pool."

Think about that—an activity that not only gets a family to hang out together, but it also occupies them enough to keep the biggest screen in the house off.

Now let me interject: I don't have a swimming pool. I wish I did, but I don't. We've never had one.

But when my friend Eric told me this, I looked at my budget to see if there was any way to make it possible. Luckily for me, my parents moved less than a mile from us and put in a nice swimming pool. So our family began spending a lot of time in their backyard. And, interestingly enough, whenever our family goes over there and hangs by the pool

- devices are accessed very little,
- we play a lot, and
- when we aren't swimming or playing, we sit around and talk.

The pool is one of those amazing arenas where communication is cultivated.

Yes, I know that a swimming pool is a huge budget item, but take this from a guy who does not own a pool. We used my parents' house as a family hangout spot all through my kids' teen years, and it was by far one of the most effective "communication arenas."

In fact, the kids would often invite their friends over to hang out for the day over at "Papa and Nana's" house, and I saw the same effect. Instead of lounging on the couch staring at their phones, kids would swim and lay out. Did they check their phones throughout the day? Absolutely. But their time spent on devices was easily cut in half, if not more.

Why?

Because they were in a fun setting surrounded by people they liked talking with.

Think about it. Young people's love for technology is much more than a love for digital circuitry; it's a tool for connection and play. If you can provide settings that deliver both of those elements, then they don't have as big a need to check their devices.

Maybe you don't have a pool, but you have other fun activities in your backyard:

- A grill where you can have family barbecues
- Outdoor games
- A zip line
- A hot tub
- Pets (more on that in the next chapter)

When you provide your kids with arenas where they can connect and have fun without their devices, you'll begin to notice screen time shrink—not disappear, but shrink.

Are you providing those kinds of arenas?

Questions to ponder:

- What kind of arenas have you provided where kids played and connected? How did that work for you?

- Is there something else you could use or create to provide this kind of arena? What would it take to do this?

- What do you think your kids get out of using their devices as much as they do? Is there a way you can provide some of the same things without their devices?

46 The New Puppy

Do you know what's almost more difficult than raising a toddler?

Raising a puppy!

Last Thanksgiving we got a brand-new puppy. Our family dog had passed away after a quick battle with lymphoma, and the kids were begging us to get a new dog. We knew a new dog meant potty training, leash training, kennel training—and money every time we did any of those things. But the McKees have always been dog people, so we got a seven-week-old goldendoodle named Pippin.

Goldendoodles are a mix between a golden retriever and a poodle. They're all the joys of a golden, without the shedding— at least that's what we were told. Sure, he doesn't shed, but he's the most hyper dog we've ever had, and we've had eight.

The biggest ordeal was the potty training. I can't believe how much this dog peed. We would take this little guy to potty, and a minute later he was squatting by our fireplace. We cleaned up a dozen puddles a day for weeks. So much work!

Which is exactly why a pet will help your family connect.

Think about it. Today's families are slowly becoming overtaken by entertainment media and technology. Kids are spending six to nine hours a day looking at screens and tuning out the family.

A pet may just be the remedy you're looking for.

First, most kids would love a pet. Say the words *kitten* or *puppy*, and a lot of kids brighten up. They love the idea.

Just *don't* make the mistake of bringing a puppy home and

surprising the family with it. This takes the power of ownership away from your kids.

I can't emphasize this enough: your kids *need* to own the decision. If you want a new puppy or kitten, dangle the idea out there and then play hard to get. Find a way of bringing it up without them knowing you are considering a new puppy.

"Did you hear that the Claneys got a new puppy?"

"Yes. I wish we could get a new puppy!"

They would probably expect you to say, "No way!" Instead, give them this: "Well, puppies take a ton of care and attention. We couldn't possibly get a puppy unless everyone agreed to pitch in and care for the little guy."

Many kids will jump on this opportunity: "You mean if we all agree to help, we can get a puppy?"

Still, play hard to get: "I don't know. We'd have to talk about it. You'd have to really all be excited about it and commit to taking care of it. A puppy is a lot of work."

If your kids are still excited about it, then begin the process of looking.

When we did this, two of our kids were excited about it, and one wasn't. But after we began looking at puppies, the third became engrossed in the process. It's hard to turn down the draw of an adorably snuggly little puppy (at least until he pees on your down comforter).

Once you get a puppy, the benefits are worth the trials and investment. For example, puppies need to be walked. You can try getting the entire family to take the dog on a walk. If you have older teens, "the family walk" might not be such a draw. But if they've owned into the decision to get a dog, then they need to at least take turns walking it. And when they do, simply join them on their walk. Walks provide uninterrupted one-on-one time with your kids, while their hands are occupied holding the leash.

Puppies also require cleaning, feeding, and, for some

breeds, grooming. Join your kids in these chores. Cleaning or grooming can take anywhere from thirty minutes to a couple of hours. Again—hands occupied—caring for the dog. Perfect connection time with your kids.

Pets can be fun companions, but better yet, they can be an excuse to hang out with your kids as they learn a responsibility.

So which is it? A puppy or a kitten? (Puppies require more work—more chances to connect with your kids.)

Questions to ponder:

- Would your kids want a new puppy?

- Would they own the decision with you?

- How could you use moments like walking or grooming the dog as a communication arena?

The "Don't" Fast

"Put your phone away!"

"Don't sit in your room staring at that phone all day!"

"Haven't you spent enough time on that device today?"

If you're the parent of a teenager and you haven't said any of the above, congratulations! (And what is your secret?)

Frankly, no matter how well behaved your kids are, no matter how much you talk with them about being responsible with their phones, you probably still use one of those phrases—*weekly!*

My kids have heard me teach this stuff in school assemblies and parent workshops literally across the world, and I still have to ask them at times, "Can you please put your phone away?" (My wife had to ask Ashley to do it recently, when they were wrapping presents together.)

Sadly, some parents get so caught up in regularly barking, "Don't even pull that phone out!" that they become the drill sergeant parent, a mere disciplinarian, and they miss out on the opportunity to connect with their kids.

Remember, parents need to practice both *bonding* and *boundaries* with their kids. If all we ever do is bark out *boundaries*, we'll hinder the opportunities to *bond*.

This sounds great in theory, but what does it truly look like in practice? In other words, how can we avoid just barking, "Don't!" at our kids, especially when it seems like today's kids spend more time staring at their phones than not staring at them?

Try a "Don't" fast for a day.

If your kid has been sitting on the couch for an hour staring at his phone and laughing, instead of saying, "Don't sit there staring at your phone all day!" just smile and nicely ask, "What are you laughing at?"

By asking your kids to share with you, you are choosing *bonding* over *boundaries* for that particular moment. You are choosing to hang out with them, maybe even laughing at a funny video, instead of correcting them for spending too much time on their devices.

Does this mean you should never say, "Don't"?

Far from it. Parents need to provide both *bonding* and *boundaries*. This "Don't" fast is just a good discipline for parents if they find themselves erring too far on the side of *boundaries*. Our kids need *bonding* as much as they need *boundaries*.

Try the "Don't" fast for a day. Then ask yourself:

- How hard was it to put off correcting them?
- Did they *really* need correction at that moment?
- How successful was my attempt at *bonding*?
- Have I erred on the side of *boundaries* too much lately? Has that hurt my attempts at *bonding*?

Questions to ponder:

- Do you find yourself having to correct your kids often about their devices?

- How do they typically respond?

- Which do you gravitate toward more: *bonding* or *boundaries*?

- Do you need to make an adjustment? What would that look like?

Caramel apples? The pumpkin patch? Fresh apple pie? Pony rides? The Christmas tree farm?

These kinds of traditions are an easy sell for young kids.

"Who wants to go to the pumpkin patch?"

"Yaaaay!"

But try the same things with your teenagers, and they may look at like you're an idiot.

That's why it's great to start these traditions when your kids are young. Think about it. If families drive up to the Christmas tree farm *every year*, get hot cocoa, stop at the special tourist trap and buy a Christmas ornament—then even teenagers may protest if you try to skip that tradition one year.

My daughter Ashley is the Christmas drill sergeant in our house. When the kids were young, we started the tradition of getting a Christmas tree and decorating it the day after Thanksgiving. Now if we try to detour from that plan in the slightest, the Christmas drill sergeant reprimands the whole family. Every year, she is the one who pulls out the boxes of decorations, puts on her favorite Christmas playlist, and announces, "Come on, everyone! Time to start decorating!"

These days are full of interactions and conversation. Technology rarely gets in the way.

These traditions and activities aren't limited to Christmas. One of our family's favorite places to visit in October and November is a place called Apple Hill.

Apple Hill is where people of the greater Sacramento area go to for the best homemade pies, berry picking, apple orchards, vineyards, and more! Families go together to pick apples, shop for crafts or visit a pumpkin patch, or even to chop down their Christmas tree. If it's crafty or delicious, Apple Hill has it.

My guess is, even if you aren't from Sacramento, you probably have a place like this near you. Whenever we visit my wife's parents in the Phoenix area, they always take us to a creative mecca of crafts and candies. It's designed like an old western town and offers all kinds of delicious goodies. My friends in Colorado took us to a similar place. Most states have them. If you don't know where they are, just find the nearest grandma wearing a sweater with a moose embroidered on the front of it and ask her.

My teenagers still love Apple Hill. In fact, many of their friends go there with their families. We've actually introduced several of their friends to the experience, and now they love going.

Who doesn't like fresh fudge or apple pie à la mode?

Plus, Apple Hill just happens to have a lousy cell signal. Bonus!

Sticky, caramel-coated fingers and a bad cell signal are just what today's parents need to keep smartphone-obsessed kids from burying their faces in their phones.

But yes, if your teenagers have never been to one of these kinds of places, it may be difficult trying to persuade them to go to events like the Greenville Badger Festival. So do what all parents of teenagers need to do: sweeten the pot, and then make them go.

"This Saturday the family is going to the Central Valley Soupfest and Frog Races. Invite a friend if you want. We're also gonna hit the Nike Outlet and Gino's Pizza on the way home."

Use whatever you need to make the day as least miserable as possible, and if your teenager isn't being a pill, maybe he or she will actually enjoy it.

Like many parenting practices, the earlier you start them, the less sugar it takes for the medicine to go down.

Questions to ponder:

- What family traditions or ventures do your kids enjoy?

- Do these adventures provide fun bonding experiences and memories for your family?

- How can you use these kinds of activities to create conversation?

49   Guys' Night/Girls' Night

Last year I asked my brother Thom if he could connect with me on a Thursday the following week. He told me, "Sorry, that's Guys' Night."

Thom wasn't talking about poker and cigars with his friends; he was talking about time with Aidan, his nine-year-old son.

Once a week, Thom and Aidan have "Guys' Night." They watch guy movies, eat guy foods, and do guy things.

Guess who loves it?

I can't get through a conversation with Aidan without him talking about "Guys' Night."

"Last week at Guys' Night, we watched. . ."

"Yesterday at Guys' Night, we went to. . ."

For Aidan, it doesn't get much better than Guys' Night.

What does your kid look forward to with you?

I admit, when my brother first started this tradition, I thought, *Why didn't I think of that?* I'd had occasional Guys' Nights with my son, but it wasn't a regular gig.

What a brilliant practice to begin when our kids are young.

My wife has accomplished this with our girls. No fancy name required—she actually calls it "Girls' Night." And it always involves chocolate and then some chick flick like *Pride and Prejudice* or binge-watching *Downton Abby* (and whining that the series isn't on anymore). And, funny enough, she didn't start this practice with them until their teen years, and she did it even more often when their older brother left for college. It's been fun for me to see the girls connecting and enjoying girl talk.

Now they almost pride themselves with the exclusivity. My girls will jokingly put their noses in the air as they march off down the hallway with Mom, telling me, "We're going to watch *Emma* with Mom."

I'll sneer and retort, "Well I'm going to eat a plate of hot wings and watch the game." (I talk tough, but now that the girls are off to college, I will often find myself enjoying a romantic comedy wiht Lori. *While You Were Sleeping* is our favorite.)

Our kids need positive adult role models who don't just talk, but who also demonstrate how to be a man or how to be a woman. Guys' Night is a great time of bonding, but also a great time for guys to talk about what it means to be a man. Guys' Night provides your boys with an arena where they know they can ask questions that may be embarrassing to ask around the girls. Girls' Night provides the same with Mom.

I've had many single-parent friends ask me, "As a single mom, how can I provide this with my son?" If Dad isn't in the picture, I encourage Mom to look for positive male role models, such as Grandpa, an uncle, or the youth pastor at the church. In my twenty-plus years of youth ministry, I was that male role model for many young men whose moms were doing amazing jobs raising them but cherished the opportunity to have a man in their kids' lives as well.

Is it too late to start Guys' Night or Girls' Night in your home?

How about this Thursday?

Questions to ponder:

- Do you have a regular time scheduled with your son or daughter?

- What would this look like?

- How could you initiate it?

- If you're a single parent, who is a positive role model you could ask to help you with this?

50 The Number Two Pastime

In 2015 Nielsen surveyed young people and asked them their favorite pastime. Can you guess their number one answer?

Listening to music.

That didn't surprise me.

But I bet you'll never guess number two.

Reading.

Yes, reading beat watching TV, social media, and playing video games.

This survey isn't the only one to reveal young people's love for reading. Common Sense Media did a similar survey, asking both tweens (eight to twelve years old) and teens (thirteen to eighteen) their favorite entertainment media activity (entertainment media actually includes reading). For tweens, reading was second, just under playing video games and above watching TV. For teens, reading was tied with social media for third, under listening to music and playing video games.

Some people would be quick to guess that the smartphone is slowly pushing aside the book. And we'd be fools to deny the draw of technology. But at the same time, today's young people love fiction.

Blame it on J. K. Rowling, because in the late nineties, reading was dying until Harry Potter changed everything. No one can pinpoint the exact tipping point when the book went viral, but when the seventh and final volume, *Harry Potter and the Deathly Hallows*, was published on July 21, 2007, it was the fastest-selling book on record, moving eleven million copies in twenty-four hours.

Reading actually became a fad—for young people! Now we are raising a generation of readers.

Are you using this as an opportunity to set technology aside and read?

When I was a kid, my parents would read The Chronicles of Narnia to us after dinner. My brother and I were pretty hyper, so they'd only read a few pages at a time, usually stopping when we still wanted more. It took us years to get through that whole series.

My wife and I decided to pass on that tradition to our kids. My kids were a little better behaved than my brother and me, so we typically read a chapter at a time.

Our reading didn't stop there. We actually read through some of the Bible as well. Genesis, 1 and 2 Samuel, Acts. The kids weren't cheering every time we whipped out a Bible after dinner, but now they look back and tell us they're glad we did it.

Don't hesitate to encourage reading on No-Tech Tuesdays, if you choose to adopt that idea. Our family would often sit around reading or doing homework, since all technology was turned off. It's a bizarre sight, seeing a family all sitting around with actual books in their hands. A flashback to a different era.

If your kids aren't big readers, search for a subject they enjoy. That's why I wrote *The Zombie Apocalypse Survival Guide for Teenagers*. That book has attracted a lot of nonreaders. Not to mention, it has discussion questions at the end of each chapter so parents can talk through the book with their teens after each chapter.

Don't underestimate the draw of reading. A good book may be just what you need to motivate your kids to put their phones down and enjoy a quiet evening with the family.

Questions to ponder:

- What book did you enjoy as a kid? Have you ever talked with your kids about this book?

- Is there a book that your kids have thoroughly enjoyed? Is that book part of a series?

- What would it take for you to initiate a time of reading (No-Tech Tuesday) with your family?

News Talk

So much of this book has been about arenas of communication, settings where conversations take place. But even if we create some of these settings, what are some creative ways to instigate conversation?

Sure, we've already discussed fingertip questions we can ask on the fly, and this book has already provided a bunch of them. But what are some other ways to jump-start conversation night after night at dinner and in many of these unique settings where the phone is actually put away?

Have you tried using the newspaper?

No, I don't want you to roll it up and smack your kids with it. The news is full of articles, stories, and studies about real life. It provides plenty of opportunities to do what you've learned in this book: share a story and then ask, "Was he right?"

As you read through your morning paper or Yahoo News feed, earmark articles you can use.

As I read through the paper recently, I found an article about the lack of exercise among American teens. In fact, just a few paragraphs into the article it revealed that only 8 percent of American kids are getting the recommended sixty minutes of exercise a day.

Wow!

That's exactly the kind of fact I would use to start a conversation with my kids. I would just read that percentage, and maybe another interesting point or two, then ask:

- Why do you think American kids aren't getting enough exercise?
- What are they doing instead?
- What do you think parents and schools should do to encourage young people toward more exercise?
- Do you think our family gets enough exercise?
- What could we do to improve this?

Notice that I didn't start with the question "Do *you* get enough exercise, you fat lard?" I started with general observations and questions about the article, then slowly moved to more personal, but never accusatory, questions.

An article can help parents in several ways:

- It gives us a springboard from which we can launch a conversation.
- It brings an expert into the room, in areas outside or beyond our expertise.
- It provides our kids with the opportunity to chime in with their opinion on various real-world issues.

If you find it difficult to get your kids engaged in these conversations, make sure you search for topics they are interested in. Better yet, find a debatable subject that may get them riled up (something we talked about in the chapter about fostering controversy). Share a controversial opinion and ask, "Is he/she right?"

If you are looking for a regular source of interesting articles to use, I provide plenty on TheSource4Parents.com. You'll find more articles than you could ever use linked in my blog, and my Youth Culture Window articles. I even have a box of links on the front of TheSource4Parents.com labeled "Offsite Articles Jonathan Has Read This Week."

Are you engaging your kids in these kinds of conversations?

Questions to ponder:

- What topics does your family typically discuss around your dinner table?

- What have you read lately that may be a good springboard for these conversations?

- How do you think your kids will respond to these kinds of discussions?

Mother's Day

"Nana needs our help."

Who's gonna argue with that?

A few years ago, my mom told all the grandkids, "Please don't give me any presents for Mother's Day. Just come over and help me plant my bulbs. Then we'll have a big barbecue."

The grandkids all happily agreed.

First, Mother's Day is in May, and Nana has an awesome backyard with a pool. Second, they love their nana. How hard can it be to help her plant some tulip bulbs?

When you picked up this book, you probably never guessed that I'd suggest "gardening with Grandma" as a way to motivate teenagers to put down their phones and participate in a family workday (which is why I saved this idea for last). But at this point in the book, you're probably getting used to the numerous approaches we can take to create these kinds of venues. In all honesty, it just takes a little bit of proactive parenting.

That's where I got myself in trouble so many times. I was *reactive* instead of *proactive*. I'd ignore my kids, they'd act out, I'd react.

If we try to put parenting on autopilot, ignoring our kids and doing the bare minimum, then they'll fill that void with entertainment media and technology. I'm not being overdramatic. Sadly, the studies are pretty clear. Most parents have given up. Most parents don't spend time or energy keeping up with their kids; instead, they just let kids do their thing. The funny thing is, these parents then complain that their kids spend too much time staring at their devices.

My guess is that you're not one of those parents.

Why?

Because you picked up this book—a book with the phrase "connect with your kid" right in the title. Maybe it's the "smartphone-obsessed kid" part that grabbed you—and that's okay. Because if you love your kids and don't want them to have an unhealthy dependency on technology, you *can* truly make a difference.

The key is being proactive.

The key is thinking ahead enough to simply plan something like a workday at Nana's house for Mother's Day so your kids may pause their technology, if only for a little while, and enjoy some gardening with Nana. Who knows, they may even keep their phone put away during the barbecue as well. If you're extremely lucky, they'll also swim in the pool. (For an annual record of two hours, thirty-eight minutes without their cell phone in one afternoon!)

All it takes is a little shrewd planning.

Go ahead. Call Grandma. She'd probably love the idea.

Questions to ponder:

- When is the last time your family worked together on a project—such as a family workday?

- Do you have a relative who could use your family's help? What could that look like?

- What other venues can you be proactive about arranging in the near future?

- What one idea in this book can you do this week?

52 Reviews & Qs

52 CREATIVE SETS OF QUESTIONS TO ASK YOUR KIDS IN THESE 52 VENUES

In the following section, you'll find a one- or two-sentence wrap-up of each chapter, with key takeaways and a handful of questions for each venue, which can help you to engage your kids in meaningful conversation.

1. The Coviewing Connection
We live in a world where kids average more than six hours a day looking at screens. Use this fact as an opportunity to connect, not to correct.

Engaging Qs:
1. If you could watch only one TV show for the next year, which would you choose? Why?
2. If you could use only one screen for the next year, which would you choose? Which screen would you miss the most?
3. Of the videos and/or shows you watch, which one do you think I'd enjoy the most? Show me.

2. The Fine Art of Shutting Up
It's amazing how much our kids are willing to talk when we create a climate in which they feel noticed and heard.

Engaging Qs:
1. If you could have lunch with anyone in the world tomorrow, who would you choose?

2. What would you want to talk about?
3. Of the people you already know, who would you want to have lunch with?

3. Fingertip Questions

Nothing opens the door to dialogue better than a well-placed question. The world provides us with plenty of teaching moments each day. Instead of lecturing our kids in these moments, ask questions. For example, if a questionable song comes on the radio, ask a question.

Engaging Qs:
1. What did he say in that chorus?
2. What does that mean?
3. Is he right? How do you know?
4. How does this mesh with your values?

4. The Teen Genius Bar

Use your kids' knowledge of technology as an opportunity to make them feel appreciated for their expertise. Ask them to help you with your technology and use that moment as a springboard for conversation.

Engaging Qs:
1. How can I block this guy from posting his spam on my timeline?
2. Have you ever had to block someone from posting something on any of your stuff?
   What's the worst thing you've seen someone post or comment on?
3. Have you ever had someone post something mean or rude about you? Tell me about it.
4. How did you handle that?
5. Would you handle it differently today?

5. The Family Docking Station

Doctors advise no phones, TVs, or Internet in the bedroom at night. Provide a family docking station where your kids can charge their phones each night safely in your bedroom. Begin this policy when they are young and first get their devices. Most kids will be very resistant to this boundary, so be ready for this discussion.

Engaging Qs:

1. Why do you think doctors advise no phones, Internet, or TV in the bedrooms?
2. Why do young people who keep phones in their rooms get an average of an hour less sleep per night?
3. How do realistic boundaries with technology help young people?
4. What boundaries do you think would help you be responsible with your phone/tablet/laptop?

6. The Value of Noticing

Look up from your phone when your kids are around and take notice. The more we learn about our kids, the better we can connect with them.

Engaging Qs:

1. If you were going to get a $100 gift card to any store for Christmas, what store would you choose?
2. What would you buy there?
3. If you could eat dinner tonight at the place of your choice, where would it be?
4. What would you order?

7. Two-Player Mode

Two-player mode is by far one of the most effective ways to connect with young people who enjoy games—*and that's most of them.* Whenever you take the time to sit down and do something with your kids that they enjoy, you'll find conversation is a natural by-product.

Engaging Qs:
1. If you were only allowed to play one video game for the next year, which one would you choose? Show me why.
2. Describe your perfect day. What makes this day so good?
3. Who would be fun to hang out with on that day? Why?

8. The Late-Night Splurge Sensation

In a world full of disciplines, it's fun to break free of routine, splurge, and build a significant memory. Try ordering pizza at ten some night, put away all mobile devices, and just hang out together.

Engaging Qs:
1. What is one of the best memories you have in this room?
2. What made it so enjoyable?
3. What would it take to top that memory?

9. Addressing the Elephant. . .er. . .the Smartphone in the Room

When you notice smartphones and other mobile devices hindering face-to-face communication, address it creatively. Don't confront your kids and put them on the defensive; just bring up the issue and ask for their opinion.

Engaging Qs:
1. Are smartphones helping or hindering communication between young people today?
2. Describe a time when you were frustrated with

someone because that person was more interested in his or her phone than in you.

3. Do you ever get so caught up with your phone that it hinders your communication with your friends in the room? Explain.
4. How can you remedy this?

10. The House to "Hang"

Become proactive about making your house a fun and hospitable place for your kids and their friends. Your hospitality can provide a place where conversation is encouraged.

Engaging Qs:
1. What is your favorite family meal?
2. What is your favorite fast-food place?
3. What would you order there?

11. The Media-Fast Fulfillment

Attempt a media fast for one day. Shrewdly share the idea, and then ask your kids if they think it's possible. Challenge them to try it as a family for twenty-four hours.

Engaging Qs:
1. Do you think our culture has become too dependent on technology? Explain.
2. What are some disciplines or boundaries people could put on themselves to prevent this from happening?
3. What are some disciplines we could try as a family?

12. The No-Tech Tuesday Tactic

Try implementing a fast from entertainment media and technology one afternoon/evening per week and instead focus on conversation, board games, reading, or throwing the ball for the dog outside.

Engaging Qs:
1. If the world's power grid shut down, what would be the first piece of technology you'd miss?
2. What would you begin doing with your time?
3. Why don't you do more of that right now?

13. The Overnight Escape Strategy

Plan some fun overnight trips with your family. When your kids are young, they'll love the adventure. When they're older, you may need to be a little more strategic.

Engaging Qs:
1. If you could get on a plane today and fly anywhere, where would you go? Why?
2. What would you do when you got there?
3. If you could bring one person with you, who would it be? Why?

14. A New Perspective of Back Talk

Parents need to provide an atmosphere where kids can freely express their thoughts and feelings. No, this doesn't mean allowing them to be rude—it means allowing them to feel truly heard.

Engaging Qs:
1. Let's say a kid at your school sits alone for lunch every day and people from other tables make fun of him. What would most of your friends do when this happens?
2. What would you do if you were in this situation?
3. What is right? How do you know?

15. The "Yes" Factor

Next time your kids ask you to hang out with them, just say yes. This becomes so much more important as your kids reach adolescence, because chances are they'll ask you less and less.

Engaging Qs:
1. What is the most encouraging thing someone has ever told you?
2. How did that make you feel?
3. Did it change you? How?
4. What do you wish someone would notice about you, but no one seems to?
5. What do you wish your family would notice?

16. The Hot Tub Adjustment

Today's parents need to keep their eyes open for "communication arenas" where kids aren't distracted by a vibration every ten seconds. A hot tub is one of the great settings where communication is cultivated.

Engaging Qs:
1. Where is your favorite place to relax?
2. Describe what relaxing looks like for you.
3. What is an activity in your life right now that may be keeping you from relaxing?
4. Is there something in your schedule you can cut?

17. Froyo Exchanges

A frozen yogurt place is just one of the many settings where you and your kids can talk while enjoying something delicious. Food jump-starts conversation. Where are your kids most likely to open up?

Engaging Qs:
1. What are your top five favorite desserts?

2. What is your favorite treat you can stop and get on the run?
3. What is your favorite treat we make at home?

18. The Safe Source
If there's one thing that damages your efforts to connect with your kids, and that destroys any of the progress you have made, it's *freaking out*. When you overreact, it communicates one thing: *Mom or Dad is not a safe source.* Turn your overreactions into interactions.

Engaging Qs:
1. If you could have a do-over for one moment in your life, what would it be?
2. How would you change it?
3. What did you learn the first time around?

19. The Fire Pit Phenomenon
Outdoor campfires are among those settings where people experience heaping portions of God's creation and minimal influence of technology.

Engaging Qs:
1. If you could build a dream home anywhere, where would it be? Why there?
2. Describe your dream home.
3. What do you think you'd have to do to make this dream home a reality?

20. The Playlist Connection
Playlists not only provide a fun connection point for families, but they tell you a lot about a person. Resist the urge to lecture your kids about inappropriate music. If we create a comfortable climate of conversation about music, social media—any topic— then our kids will come to us again and again.

Engaging Qs:
1. Play me a song you feel like listening to right now.
2. Play me the song you play where you're sad.
3. Play me the song you play when you're happy.
4. Tell me about this song. What did the artist say?
5. What do you think the artist means?
6. Is the artist right? Explain.

21. The Serving Strategy
Look for opportunities where your family can volunteer together, serving your community. Many of these settings create opportunities for dialogue. Maximize any setting where phones stay in our pockets and we dialogue with other people face-to-face.

Engaging Qs:
1. Describe a time when you wanted to reach out and help someone in need.
2. How could you have helped?
3. What could you do today to help people in a needy situation?

22. The New Kicks Occurrence
Your kids' shoes may provide you some insight as to what they value. Today's young people often value fashion. Use that as a springboard for conversation.

Engaging Qs:
1. What are your favorite shoes?
2. Where would you wear them?
3. What is the next pair of shoes you want? Why?

23. The Hunting Hush

Hunting requires you to be in tune with your surroundings, and that usually means "no tech." Be on the lookout for settings with no cell service, beautiful surroundings, and a climate that cultivates conversation.

Engaging Qs:

1. If you could have a wild animal as a pet, what would you want?
2. What animal frightens you the most?
3. What is your favorite animal to hunt?

24. What's Your Favorite...?

Connect more than you correct. Instead of correcting your kids when they are indulging in entertainment media, use it to connect with them. Simply ask, "Show me your favorite..."

Engaging Qs:

1. Show me the funniest YouTube videos you've discovered.
2. What is your favorite meme?
3. What is your favorite Vine?
4. What is something you like to create?

25. Pocket It

In a world where many American adults actually spend more time looking at screens than at their teens, discipline yourself to put that phone aside for your family. Your actions will speak louder than your words.

Engaging Qs:

1. Where is a fun place you like to hang out with the family?
2. What do you like about this place?
3. When should we go there again?
4. Is there a similar place we could go to have a fun time?

26. The Greasy Spoon Exchange

Look for settings where your kids smile and grow chatty. Make this a place where you can connect with your kids consistently—like a weekly date.

Engaging Qs:

1. What do you eat for lunch most days at school?
2. What do you wish you could eat?
3. Does your school actually provide anything tasty?
4. What one item could you pack in your lunch that you would actually enjoy?

27. Fostering Controversy

Instead of avoiding the sticky situations that life throws at us, embrace them and use them as an opportunity to ask your kids what they would do in the situation.

Engaging Qs:

1. You go to your friend's house and they start playing a video game with highly explicit content. What do you think you should do?
2. Name a time when something like this occurred.
3. What did you do? How did that work out for you?
4. Now that you've had time to think about it, what do you think you should have done?

28. The Fan

Find an opportunity to show up, watch your kids do something they're good at, and offer some words of affirmation. It may be the only affirmation they hear all week.

Engaging Qs:

1. What is your favorite sport/instrument to play?
2. Do you see this as a fun hobby or a serious pursuit?
3. Who do you admire who is really good at this?

4. What is something you want to accomplish this year with this sport/instrument?
5. What will that require from you?

29. No Tech at the Table
Dinnertime is a no-tech zone, a precious place where your kids feel noticed and heard.

Engaging Qs:
1. What is your favorite app/website?
2. What do you like to do on this app/site?
3. How much time do you spend on this app/site each day?
4. How's that working for you?

30. Kitchen Creations
Hands that are busy cooking or baking are typically too busy to pick up a smartphone.

Engaging Qs:
1. What is your favorite thing to cook/bake?
2. What would you like to learn how to cook/bake?
3. Would you like to cook/bake this for the family sometime? When?

31. The Wings and Rings Circle
A sports bar may be yet another venue where families connect. If you discover an arena like this where your kids naturally engage in dialogue with you, jump on the opportunity to do it again.

Engaging Qs:
1. If you could go to any game from any sport, what would you want to see?
2. Who is your favorite player?
3. What do you like about him/her?
4. What player makes you angry? Why?

32. The *My Big Fat Greek Wedding* Method

Instead of telling your kids, "You should," try asking them, "Should you?" Lead them to discover the answer (just like Gus's wife led him to think he came up with the solution in *My Big Fat Greek Wedding*).

Engaging Qs:
1. Have you ever been in a situation like this before?
2. What did you do then?
3. How did that work out for you?
4. So what do you think would be best this time?

33. Netflix-Binge Bonding

Just because coviewing entertainment media involves a lot of sitting in silence, that doesn't mean it hinders bonding. Activities like this provide connection through a shared experience and are frequently followed by a time of conversation about the experience.

Engaging Qs:
1. Who is your favorite character in this show? Why?
2. Who irritates you in this show?
3. Do you know anyone like that?
4. What do you think about what he/she did?
5. Was he/she right?

34. The School Shuttle Strategy

Shuttling your kids to school each day provides yet another arena where you sit side by side with your kids, giving you an opportunity to dialogue with them.

Engaging Qs:
1. If you could have ditched all classes but one today, which class would you have actually attended? Why?

2. Who do you talk with the most in this class? Do you enjoy their company?
3. Describe your typical lunch routine.
4. What would make it better?
5. If you were stuck in an elevator with one of your teachers for a day, which teacher would you choose? Why?
6. What would you talk with the teacher about?
7. Which teacher would you hate getting stuck in an elevator with?

35. The Tandem Connection

Tandem bikes and kayaks provide a unique setting where two people always end up talking because they're mere inches from each other and there's nothing else to do.

Engaging Qs:
1. If your PE teacher let you choose one exercise to do for the entire class period, what would you choose?
2. What do you like about that exercise?
3. What is a workout or exercise you despise? Why?
4. What is a fun exercise to do with someone else?
5. Who would be your top choice to exercise with?

36. Resisting the Stalker

Today's parents need to become involved in their kids' lives enough so they get to know their world through conversation, not spying. Start strict when kids first acquire their own mobile devices; then give them an increasing amount of responsibility and freedom as they mature.

Engaging Qs:
1. Whose posts are typically your favorite on any given day on Instagram?
2. What do you like about their posts?

3. Which are your least favorite posts?
4. What irritates you about these?
5. When have you posted something and then regretted it?
6. What did you learn from that experience?

37. Under the Comforter

Take time to kiss your kids good night every night when they go to bed. Your kids typically feel safe and technology is put away, making it a great communication arena.

Engaging Qs:
1. What was the best thing that happened to you today?
2. What was the worst?
3. What is one thing you look forward to tomorrow?
4. What is one thing you don't look forward to?
5. How can I help?

38. Water Like Glass

There's something about being in the outdoors that helps kids lift their eyes from their phones and absorb the beauty of their surroundings. One of the best places to enjoy this kind of majestic isolation is from a boat gliding across smooth water. Times like these can springboard the most random conversations.

Engaging Qs:
1. What is your favorite snack at the movie theater?
2. What food should they serve in movie theaters?
3. What is the best movie you saw this year?
4. Any movies you are looking forward to?

39. The Coffeehouse Couch Connection

The typical coffeehouse provides a cozy atmosphere conducive to conversation: high-top tables, couches, tables for groups of all sizes. The setting is perfect for conversation.

Engaging Qs:
1. What is your favorite coffee shop drink?
2. What is a drink that many people like but you don't?
3. What is your typical order when you come here?
4. Do you ever change it up? How?

40. Memory Lane

Whenever you pull out old home movies of your kids when they were young, they'll typically be curious enough to sit down and watch with you for a while.

Engaging Qs:
1. If you could live in any time period, when would it be?
2. Why this time period?
3. What modern luxuries would you miss the most?
4. What wouldn't you miss?

41. Here Are the Keys

Embrace opportunities to let your kids engage in activities that demand adult responsibility in the safety of your shadow. Activities like driving the boat, operating the saw, or simply setting up the home entertainment center with you often monopolize your kids' attention and require mobile devices to be put away.

Engaging Qs:
1. If you could drive any vehicle, what would it be?
2. What kind of car/boat/motorcycle do you think you'll realistically purchase someday?
3. What is your favorite vehicle we've owned so far?
4. What's a good memory in this vehicle?

42. Peak Exchanges

Outdoor activities often have these common denominators: beautiful scenery that keeps heads up, no Wi-Fi signal, unique settings that naturally provoke conversations. Be intentional about embarking on activities, such as hiking trips, that provide these kinds of settings.

Engaging Qs:
1. What chore do you despise?
2. What do you hate about it?
3. Is there a chore you don't mind?
4. If you had to do manual labor for a living, what would you choose?
5. Is there something you'd prefer to do for a living besides manual labor?
6. What's it going to take to get there?

43. The Mani-Pedi

Make a mani-pedi appointment with your kids so you can be pampered while sitting next to each other. Hands are occupied, phones are in the pockets, and conversation is always a by-product.

Engaging Qs:
1. If you could go to any amusement park, where would you want to go?
2. What is your favorite thing to do there, or at amusement parks in general?
3. What food would you buy that day?

44. The Cookie Dough Connection

Making cookie dough together is one of those splurges that occupies hands (phones in the pocket), puts most people in a good mood, and causes conversation to flow naturally.

Engaging Qs:
1. Let's say school is canceled tomorrow. What would you do?
2. What is your favorite activity to do in the summer?
3. What is your favorite activity to do in the winter?
4. What is something we should do as a family this month?

45. Poolside Moments

Hanging out by a pool as a family provides an arena where swimming and playing usually trumps staring at mobile devices. Even if you don't have a pool (I don't), your community probably has a lake or community spot where you can lie by the water.

Engaging Qs:
1. Describe your perfect vacation.
2. What are some activities you would do on this vacation?
3. What has been your favorite family vacation?
4. Where should we go next?

46. The New Puppy

Pets are more than just fun companions; they are an excuse to hang out with your kids when they are learning the responsibility of caring for them.

Engaging Qs:
1. What kind of pet are you going to own when you get out on your own?
2. What will you name it?
3. What do you think is the best part about owning an animal like this?
4. What is the worst part?

47. The "Don't" Fast

Turn your overreaction into interaction. Instead of barking, "Don't" at your kids when they are glued to their mobile devices, just smile and nicely ask them, "Whatcha looking at?"

Engaging Qs:
1. What are you sitting there giggling at? Show me.
2. If you could have only one feature on your phone, what would you choose?
3. Which feature would you miss the most?
4. What feature is probably the best for you?
5. Which feature probably has the most potential to hinder you?

48. Tradition Momentum

Start fun family traditions when your kids are young—like visiting pumpkin patches, cutting down a Christmas tree, or visiting fun local tourist traps. These days are full of interaction and conversation.

Engaging Qs:
1. What is your favorite holiday? Why?
2. What is your favorite holiday meal?
3. What holiday tradition do you love most?
4. What holiday tradition will you probably change with your own family someday?
5. What holiday tradition should we add?

49. Guys' Night/Girls' Night

Moms and dads should try to find regular alone time with their kids. Quality time with the same-gender parent can open doors to honest conversations in which kids feel free to ask vulnerable questions.

Engaging Qs:
1. Describe your perfect spouse.
2. What qualities are nonnegotiable?

3. What doesn't matter?
4. Where will you find a person like this?
5. What qualities do you think your spouse will like about you?

50. The Number Two Pastime

Don't underestimate the draw of reading. A good book may be just what you need to motivate your kids to put their phones down and enjoy a quiet evening with the family.

Engaging Qs:

1. If you were going somewhere for a year and could only bring one book, which book would you bring? Why?
2. What is your favorite book you've ever read?
3. What did you like about it?
4. What book would you like to read but haven't?

51. News Talk

The news is full of articles, stories, and studies about real life, and they provide plenty of opportunities to do some of the things you've learned about in this book. Share a story, and then engage in conversation with your kids about it.

Engaging Qs:

1. What do you think about what the people did in this story?
2. Did they do the right things or the wrong things?
3. What would you have done?
4. How do you think it would have worked out for you?

52. Mother's Day

Use holidays like Mother's Day as a special time to pause from technology, if only for a little while, and enjoy conversation with Mom and/or Grandma.

Engaging Qs:

1. If a tornado/hurricane was heading toward our house and you only had time to fill one small duffel bag, name five items you'd be sure to grab.
2. Why these items?
3. What do you think you would have grabbed a few years ago?
4. What has changed?

SOURCES

Being Smarter Than the Smartphone
1. Common Sense Media.
https://www.commonsensemedia.org/sites/default/files/
uploads/research/census_executivesummary.pdf
2. National Sleep Foundation. https://sleepfoundation.
org/sites/default/files/2014-NSF-Sleep-in-America-poll-
summary-of-findings---FINAL-Updated-3-26-14-.pdf
3. Michigan State University Study.
http://www.thedailybeast.com/articles/2014/06/24/is-it-
time-for-a-classroom-cellphone-ban.html
4. The Source for Parents.
http://www.thesource4parents.com/YouthCultureWindow/
article.aspx?ID=290
5. Fox News.
http://www.myfox28columbus.com/news/features/top-
stories/stories/Teen-Stress-101-More-Teens-Than-Ever-
Dealing-With-Online-Bullying-56910.shtml#.VIEuejHF-So
6. The Cut.
http://nymag.com/thecut/2014/02/addicted-to-likes-social-
media-makes-us-needier.html
7. Daily Mail.
http://www.dailymail.co.uk/news/article-2583604/Social-
media-makes-teenagers-feel-like-inadequate-star-second-
rate-biopic-warns-headteacher.html
8. TNW.
http://thenextweb.com/insider/2016/01/07/the-web-is-
quietly-creating-a-generation-of-miserable-kids/
9. The Times.
http://www.thetimes.co.uk/tto/health/child-health/
article4658595.ece
10. Time.
http://time.com/2948467/chances-are-your-teen-is-sexting/

11. FYI.
http://fulleryouthinstitute.org/blog/viamedia-how-young-is-
too-young
12. Science Direct.
http://www.sciencedirect.com/science/article/pii/
S0747563214003227
13. Cyber Psychology.
http://www.cyberpsychology.eu/view.
php?cisloclanku=2013071101&article=3
14. CBC News.
http://www.cbc.ca/news/health/social-media-affecting-
teens-concepts-of-friendship-intimacy-1.2543158
15. The Daily Dot.
http://www.dailydot.com/technology/online-dating-study-
compatibility/

Chapter 1. The Coviewing Connection
1. Common Sense Media.
https://www.commonsensemedia.org/sites/default/files/
uploads/research/census_executivesummary.pdf

Chapter 5. The Family Docking Station
1. AAP Gateway.
http://pediatrics.aappublications.org/content/126/5/1012
2. Nielsen.
http://www.nielsen.com/us/en/insights/news/2012/young-
adults-and-teens-lead-growth-among-smartphone-owners.
html
3. Jonathan McKee blog.
http://www.jonathanmckeewrites.com/archive/2015/04/14/
todays-teens-tech.aspx
4. AAP Gateway.
http://pediatrics.aappublications.org/content/132/5/958
5. National Sleep Foundation.
https://sleepfoundation.org/sites/default/files/2014-NSF-
Sleep-in-America-poll-summary-of-findings---FINAL-
Updated-3-26-14-.pdf

Chapter 7. Two-Player Mode
1. Nielsen.
http://www.nielsen.com/content/dam/corporate/us/
en/reports-downloads/2015-reports/total-audience-
report-q22015.pdf
2. Common Sense Media.
https://www.commonsensemedia.org/sites/default/files/
uploads/research/census_executivesummary.pdf

Chapter 9. Addressing the Elephant. . .er. . .the Smartphone in the Room
1. Science Direct.
http://www.sciencedirect.com/science/article/pii/
S0747563214003227
2. Cyber Psychology.
http://www.cyberpsychology.eu/view
php?cisloclanku=2013071101&article=3

Chapter 14. A New Perspective of Backtalk
1. Wiley Online Library.
http://onlinelibrary.wiley.com/doi/10.1111/j.1467-
8624.2011.01682.x/abstract
2. NPR.
http://www.npr.org/blogs/health/2012/01/03/144495483/
why-a-teen-who-talks-back-may-have-a-bright-future

Chapter 25. Pocket It
1. Mashable.
http://mashable.com/2014/03/05/american-digital-media-
hours/
2. Daily Mail.
http://www.dailymail.co.uk/sciencetech/article-2577634/
Step-away-mobile-Parents-distracted-role-phones-harm-
bond-child.html
3. NY Times.
http://www.nytimes.com/2015/09/27/opinion/sunday/stop-
googling-lets-talk.html?_r=1

Chapter 29. No Tech at the Table
1. CASA.
http://www.casacolumbia.org/addiction-research/reports/
importance-of-family-dinners-2012

Chapter 33. Netflix-Binge Bonding
1. AAP Gateway.
http://pediatrics.aappublications.org/content/132/5/958.full

Chapter 36. Resisting the Stalker
1. The Source for Parents.
http://www.thesource4parents.com/YouthCultureWindow/
article.aspx?ID=290

Chapter 50. The Number-Two Pastime
1. MediaPost.
http://www.mediapost.com/publications/article/264073/its-
all-about-age.html
2. Common Sense Media.
https://www.commonsensemedia.org/sites/default/files/
uploads/research/census_executivesummary.pdf
3. The Wall Street Journal.
http://www.wsj.com/articles/SB10001424052702304584004
576419742308635716

Chapter 51. News Talk
1. The News & Observer.
http://www.newsobserver.com/living/family/
article48577665.html